PURE STYLE

PURE STYLE

JANE CUMBERBATCH

PHOTOGRAPHY BY

HENRY BOURNE

STEWART,
TABORI
& CHANG

Art Director **Jacqui Small**

Art Editor **Penny Stock**

Senior Editor **Sian Parkhouse**

Project Editor **Sophie Pearse**

Stylist **Jane Cumberbatch**

Assistant Stylist **Fiona Craig McFeeley**

Production **Vincent Smith**

DTP Manager **Caroline Wollen**

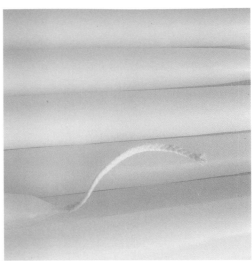

Text © Jane Cumberbatch 1996
Design and photographs
© 1996 Ryland Peters & Small
Cavendish House, 51-55 Mortimer Street
London W1N 7TD

Published in 1996 and distributed in the U.S. by
Stewart, Tabori & Chang,
a division of U.S. Media Holdings, Inc.
575 Broadway, New York, NY 10012

Distributed in Canada by
General Publishing Company Ltd.
30 Lesmill Road, Don Mills, Ontario
Canada M3B 2T6

Library of Congress Catalog Card
Number: 96-68265

ISBN: 1-55670-489-5

Produced by Mandarin Offset
Printed in Hong Kong
10 9 8 7 6 5 4 3 2 1

Contents

INTRODUCTION

Pure Style is not just about rooms and furnishings, or about trying to create an impossibly perfect glossy lifestyle. *Pure Style* is about trying to create a balance. It's about making life luxurious, not in a costly, glitzy sense, but in a more matter-of-fact, practical and natural way. *Pure Style* is about paring down and trying to live with less clutter (the fewer things we have to fuss about, the more we can get on with living). It's about simple, basic design that combines function and beauty of form to create a look that is crisp, clean, classic, and timeless.

PURE STYLE IS

being economical without skimping on essential things like good food or a decent bed. *Pure Style* is not concerned with slavishly following fashions in interiors; it's about being practical and resource-ful—tracking down great domestic staples that have been around a long time, using the high street chain stores for good basic buys, or seeking out secondhand furniture that can be revitalized with a coat of paint. *Pure Style* focuses on the sensual side of living: such as texture—sudsy soap, rough log baskets, string bags, a twiggy wreath entwined with fresh rosemary sprigs, or the bliss of sleeping in pure white cotton sheets; scents—fresh flowers, scented candles or laundry aired outside in

the hot sun; tastes—good bread or new potatoes cooked with fresh mint; color—light, bright, airy, matte shades inspired by nature as found in Queen Anne's Lace, egg and calico whites, butter and straw yellows, bean greens, sea and sky blues, and earth tones; natural things—moss, lichen, shells, pebbles; smells—great coffee, chocolate, and delicious wine; fabrics—good value, durable, and decorative, in simple patterns like checks and stripes; basics—functional items that look good, such as a tin mug, a pudding basin, or glass mason jars. *Pure Style* is about creating living, breathing spaces throughout the house. This book shows you how to be functional and practical in the kitchen, with durable counters, proper cupboards, and the essential kitchen utensils. *Pure Style* is about making the rituals of eating as sensual as is practical or possible and shows how simple elements—white plates, starched linen, and jars of cut flowers—can create pleasing and visually satisfying table arrangements. *Pure Style* also demonstrates how plain but delicious basic ingredients—good cheese, fresh fish, best quality fruit and vegetables—are the key to hassle-free food preparation. For the sitting room, *Pure Style* illustrates how a combination of elements and textures, such as comfortable seating, beautiful fabrics in cotton, wool and muslin, and candlelight and blazing fires, help to make a room relaxing and peaceful. To help you slumber more soundly, *Pure Style* shows you the benefits of well-made beds and proper mattresses as well as the luscious qualities of crisp cotton bedlinen, snuggly warm woollen blankets, and quilts. For the bathroom, this book demonstrates how lots of piping hot water, together with soft cotton towels and wonderful soaps, make bathing a truly pleasurable experience.

ELEMEN

T S

To touch, to hold, to look, to smell, to taste: the sensual aspects of life are there to be nurtured and enjoyed. Engage the senses and explore the visceral elements around you. Douse your sensibilities with tactile elements: incorporate inspiring colors and textures into your home to make life an altogether more spirited and rewarding affair.

Color

Use color to make daily living more pleasurable and uplifting. Thinking about how color appears in nature gives clues to choosing the sorts of colors you might want to have in your home. Neutrals are timeless and easy to live with, while white is unifying, restful, and a favorite with those who seek a simple approach to living. Greens are versatile, ranging from the brightest lime to much subtler tones, and earthy hues of brown can be used for a variety of looks. The sea and sky colors found in denim, on china, bedlinen, and in paint give clarity and crispness to interior settings. Look at garden borders to appreciate the range of pinks and transfer these indoors as soft lilac walls or muted floral cottons. Creams and yellows are cheerful, optimistic colors and have universal appeal. *Pure Style* is not about slavishly coordinated color schemes, although it does show you how to put together rooms and interiors with accents on color. It is more about considering the colors around us and incorporating them into our daily lives. Color is a vital element in characterizing an interior and it need not be expensive. If you cannot afford a complete redecoration, subtly change the emphasis with different pillows, covers, and splashes of floral detail.

Whites

Milk

Egg White

Wax White

Bone

Oatmeal

Muslin

Brilliant white, eggshell white, bone white, limestone white, and even plain old white, are just some examples of the plethora of available contrasting white hues and tones. White creates a peaceful and timeless ambience that benefits both period and starker contemporary settings. It is a minimalist's dream shade and makes for harmonious, unifying spaces. In today's super-charged, technical world it's good for the soul to retreat into a reviving white oasis where simplicity rules. For an all-white scheme, strip and then paint floorboards in white floor paint and seal with a yacht varnish; use white emulsion on the walls and ceilings. So that the whole interior does not look too much like the inside of a refrigerator, create tonal contrasts by giving the woodwork

hints of off-white, bone, or white with gray. For a unifying effect, paint furniture in similar shades and add cotton drill slip-on covers, muslin pillows and diaphanous gauze drapes. Complete the look with accessories such as white china and bedlinen, available from big department stores at bargain prices during the sales.

Blues

Blue spans a host of color variations, from deep hyacinth to very pale ice-blue. It can turn to lavender when mixed with violet, and turquoise when blended with green. ·In the middle of the spectrum are the purer blues of bachelor's buttons and bright powder blue. Take a cue from the fashion world and look at the soft blues that characterize denim as it is washed and worn. These shades adapt as easily to home furnishings as they do to jeans and jackets. Pale shades are the tones most likely to appear cold, especially in north-facing rooms. The trick here is to use warming devices, such as faded kelims or terra-cotta flowerpots, perhaps in a room with duck-egg blue walls. If a pure blue is too strong for your taste, try a duller mix of gray, green, and blue. This works well with highlights of white: try a dining room scheme in a subdued blue, offset with white-painted furniture, blue-and-white check curtains, and bowls of white narcissi. For a more homespun look, combine the muted Shaker blues with red-and-white striped or

Washed Blue

Sea

Beach-hut Blue

Denim

Checked Blue

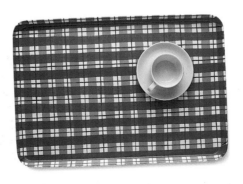

checked cotton. Useful decorating details in blue include tartan china and clear blue glass. There is blue-and-white ticking for loose covers and storage bags. For a jaunty beach-house theme, make up chair covers in bright lavender blue, cricket-stripe cotton, and faded blue-jean cotton pillows (various denim weights are available from fabric wholesalers).

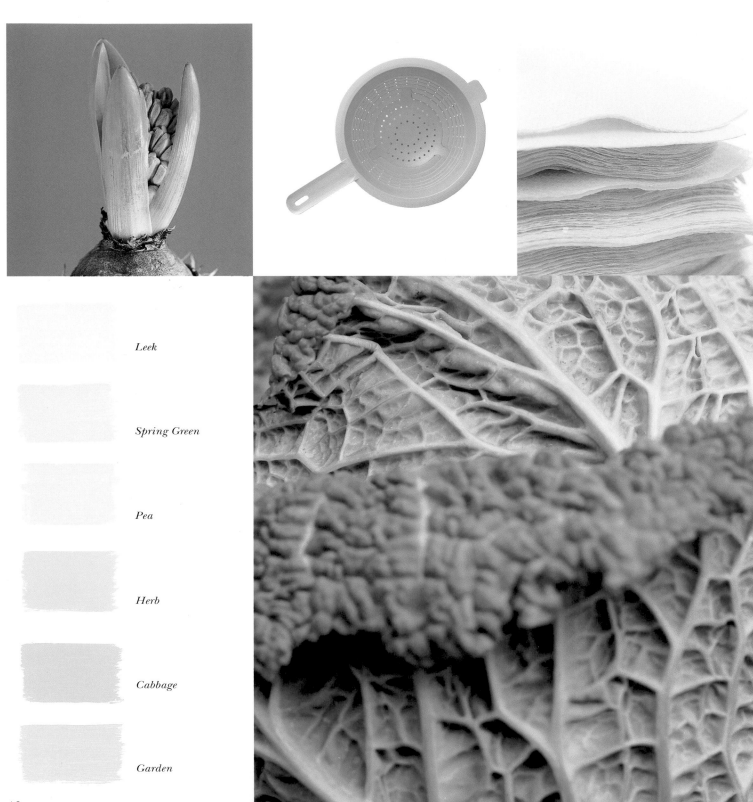

Leek

Spring Green

Pea

Herb

Cabbage

Garden

Green

Green is one of the most accommo-dating colors for interiors. In a contemporary setting a vivid apple-green or lime teamed with flourishes of fuchsia pink can work well, while traditional interiors call for duller shades mixed with gray, such as hop-sack and olive. Take inspiration from the range of greens in nature; look at the lime-green stems of hyacinths or the blades of fresh spring grass. Peas in their pods and cabbage leaves provide another source of vibrant and sometimes variegated greens. Try using sage-and-white striped cotton for chair covers with bursts of lime green for pillows.

Pink and Lavender

Pink does not need to be a sickly color associated with frilly, little-girl bedrooms, over-the-top chintzy floral drawing rooms, or the monotonous peach-colored bathrooms that are perennial in mass-produced home design catalogs. At the other extreme, shocking-pink walls and ceilings are hardly a recipe for subtle, under-stated living. Careful selection and combinations of pinks with other colors are therefore the key to mak-ing a stylish, comfortable statement. In contemporary settings, fuchsia pink, lavender, and green combine well—just look to the flowerbeds outside for inspiration and think of purple lavender heads on sage-green foliage or foxglove bells with bright green stalks and leaves. For a stylish, modern scheme for a living room paint the walls white, cover the chairs in pale lavender, and make up pillows in plain fuchsia and lime-green cot-tons. Hot pink floral prints look great married to white walls and white slip covers, creating a fresh, crisp look.

More delicate pink schemes need careful consideration to avoid looking bland. For a pink, though not at all prissy bedroom, paint walls a warm shade such as a pale rose with a hint of brown and furnish the room with a lavender-colored antique patchwork quilt and muslin Roman blinds—the whole effect will be clean and subtle with the added touch of color.

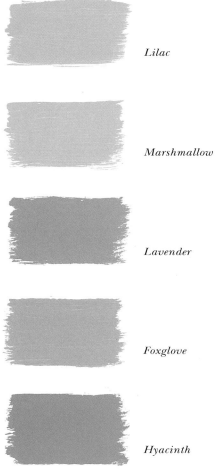

Lilac

Marshmallow

Lavender

Foxglove

Hyacinth

On the culinary front, think of enticing, deep pink, fresh strawberry ice cream; sticky and spongy marshmallows and violet-cream candies. Less threatening to body shape are pink turnips, rhubarb, radiccio leaves, and even pink pasta. For bright detail try adding smooth plastic objects in pink, such as mugs, brushes, and buckets.

21

Earth and Terra Cotta

Brick

Clay

Coir

Sack

Chocolate

Because earthy hues are universally adaptable base colors it is hard to go wrong with them, except for those really drab, mud-colored schemes that were so popular during the Seventies. Ranging from dark chocolate to cream, brown accents work well in both rustic and contemporary settings. Consider the terra cotta-

colored façades that are prevalent throughout Provençe and Spain, the brown woodwork and detailing of an English cottage kitchen, or the terra-cotta flagstones and wooden beams in a New England farmhouse. In contrast, imagine a white, utilitarian, urban loft with schoolhouse-style, dark wooden desks, tables, chairs, and filing cabinets. Study the shades of

soil, from a clay-based red to a rich, dark brown, and see how they act as a foil for brighter colors in nature. Clay pots are perfect for setting off the foliage and flowers of emerging spring bulbs. Be bold with earthy tones. For instance, paint a dining room in a rich Etruscan shade for a warm effect both night and day. Even boring beige is still a favorite shade and fabric companies love it for its versatility. Beige looks smart in various clever contemporary reworkings such as coir and natural fiber matting for floors, tough neutral linen for curtains and chair covers, or brown office files and filing boxes. Use striped and checked cotton in pinkish terra cotta and white to give chair covers and curtains a wonderfully natural feel.

Yellow

Creamy yellows, reminiscent of the countryside, are wonderfully adaptable and increase the sense of space in cramped and darkened rooms. When decorating, opt for the softer end of the yellow spectrum as acidic yellows are harder to live with because of their sharpness. However, do not go too pale, as at the other end of the scale, very clear, light primrose shades can appear insipid. Creams and yellows look great with white or even orange. Some shades look much darker in the paint can, but once on the walls are wonderfully rich and very well-suited to period hallways and kitchens. A slightly more acidic yellow will be lighter yet still rich in color and should look good in artificial light and really glowing when the sun shines. There are also some very rich, bright yellows available. If you can withstand their intensity, these strong shades will illuminate and cheer up even the smallest spaces and look fabulous against blue-and-white china and furnishings. Cream or yellow paint looks good on walls and as a decorative color for furniture.

In a cream-colored kitchen, choose traditional stone bowls and white dishes to suit the simple theme. In living rooms, yellow walls look good against mustard-colored checked and plain cottons, with contrasting details in terra cotta or blue. Yellows really come into their own in springtime when rooms are filled with daffodils and other flowers.

Butter

Honey

Pudding Basin

Straw

Mustard

Texture

Scant attention is paid to our senses by the purveyors of today's technological gadgetry with their ever-increasing obsession for convenience and labor-saving devices. There is not much textural appeal, for example, about computer hardware, or mass-produced, static-inducing synthetic carpets and fabrics. In complete contrast, sensual textures like soft wool blankets, crisp cotton bedlinens, and light and downy pillows are staples handed down from past genera-tions that help to bolster us against the more soulless elements of modern living. From the perfect smoothness of a baby's skin to the gnarled and ridged bark on a tree, natural textures are there for us to notice and appreciate. They often combine an alluring mix of qualities. For instance, lumps of volcanic pumice stone, logs, and shells are defined as rough or smooth, depending on the degree of erosion upon them by wind, sun, fire, and rain. It is this very naturalness that compels us to gather such things for the house. Our homes need natural textures to transform them into living breathing spaces. Polished wooden floors, rough log baskets, and pure cotton fabrics are just some of the organic items that we can introduce to suggest this enriching effect.

Smooth

Smooth objects are often fresh and clean and appear all around the house, especially in the kitchen and bathroom. Washing activities spring to mind, such as a handful of foaming soap or a big plastic bucketful of hot soapy water. The satisfyingly smooth surfaces of white tiling and marble or utilitarian stainless steel conjure up a sense of clinical, streamlined efficiency. In kitchens, culinary preparation is made more efficient and hygienic when work surfaces can easily be rinsed, wiped, and made pristine. Utensils such as sparkling stainless-steel pots and pans also help to keep culinary tasks running smoothly. I love to cook with a selection of worn wooden spoons which have somehow molded to my grip after years of devoted use.

Smooth, cast-iron bathtub surfaces and ceramic tiled walls can be scoured and scrubbed so helping to keep bathrooms squeaky clean. Indoors as well as out, natural surfaces such as slate or well-worn flags are texturally pleasing. Smooth elements exist in a diversity of guises, from soft white tissue paper tied up with silk ribbon to polished floorboards. On the theme of food, smooth goodies include wonderfully slippery waxed paper that gourmet shops wrap cheese in, slender glass bottles of olive oil, or slivers of fine chocolate in layers of the thinnest silver paper. You can bring naturally smooth objects indoors for textural decoration, such as ancient weathered pebbles and scoured driftwood picked up on a beach hunt.

Rough

One of my favorite possessions is a roughly hewn, olive-wood basket from Spain. Made from the winter prunings of olive trees it is silvery-gray in color, robust in design, and a sheer pleasure to touch and hold. The locals in Spain use such baskets to transport eggs, wild mushrooms, oranges, or tomatoes from their vegetable patches, while mine is filled with kindling for the fireplace. Rough, tough, and hairy flooring in sisal and coir is durable and, even when woven into patterns, it still looks like a natural texture.

Equally, a rough terra cotta-tiled floor is not only satisfying to walk on but also has the appearance of having been in place forever if its tiles are not laid in exact uniformity.

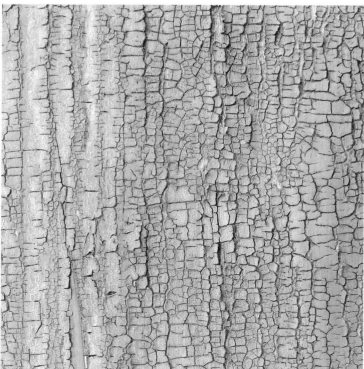

Rough textures in nature have usually been created by the elements, and even sun-blistered paint, (a painter and decorator's nightmare,) can create a visually pleasing finish on a weathered old shed. This sense of roughness allied to age means that unevenly plastered or whitewashed walls or features such as battered tongue-and-groove paneled doors can make even a new house look rustic. Rough can mean contemporary too, and utilitarian concrete walls and floors are common features in industrial buildings converted into open, loft-style living spaces.

Roughness is not always a pleasing texture, as anyone with chapped hands or prickly wool next to the skin knows, yet some fabrics such as cotton towels worn rough by repeated washing are perfect for an exhilarating rubdown after a shower. Tools such as pumice stones and hard bristle brushes assist exfoliation and improve circulation.

Scent and Taste

Scents and tastes are so evocative that childhood memories may be unexpectedly recalled by a certain waft of perfume or the aroma of a particular food. As a small girl on vacation in continental hotels, I invariably associated France with a cocktail of scents that included furniture polish, smelly plumbing, and cooked garlic. In the same way, the first sweet grass clippings of spring, evident as I pass by a newly mown field, park, or suburban backyard, transport me back to games played on the lawn at my grandmother's house in the country. Smells quicken our senses, increase anticipation, and act as powerful stimuli—there is nothing like the whiff of strong coffee and toast to entice slothful risers out of bed. Taste is crucial to the pleasure we take in eating. In addition to a knowledge and appreciation of basic cooking skills, fresh ingredients are vital if food is to taste good,. There is a world of difference between a homemade hamburger and the cardboard creations served at fast-food chains. Smell and taste are closely related, and one without the other would diminish the intensity of many eating experiences. Consider the first strawberry of the summer; its heady, flowery scent is a beguiling hint of the sweetness that is to follow.

Flavor and Fragrance

It is invigorating to have good smells around the house. I love paper-white narcissi, whose flowers emit the most delicious sweet smell. Scented candles and bowls of potpourri are other sources of floral scents. In the kitchen, scents and tastes come to the fore: the fragrant citrus tang of grated lemon peel accompanies the preparation of sauces and desserts and the

earthy scent of wild mushrooms being fried rapidly in butter is any food lover's idea of heaven. Simple tastes are often the most sublime. What could be more enticing than a bowl of pasta mixed with garlic and a little olive oil, or a good, strong cheese? Herbs such as basil, rosemary, thyme, and dill smell delicious and help to draw out the flavors of food.

Fabrics

Setting taste and aesthetic considerations aside, the criteria for choosing one type of furnishing fabric over another include the suitability of the weight and weave for a particular type of furnishing and the fabric's ability to withstand the effects of everyday wear and tear. Cotton, linen, wool, silk, synthetic, and mixed fibers for furnishing exist in a wealth of colors, textures, and weights, and with a little effort it should be possible to find just about anything you want at a price you can afford. If you fall for a really expensive fabric that is over your budget, invest in a small amount for a pillow or two instead. Otherwise, it's worth hunting around at a sale for the larger quantities needed for upholstery. For good value basics, go to an old-fashioned fabric store and track down companies who supply the television, film, theater, and art trades. These are great places to find varied weights of muslin, such as those used for toiles in the fashion business, or extra-wide widths of canvas used as stage backdrops and cheap rolls of gauze employed by designers for sets and costumes. One popular silk specialist I know carries a vast stock of colored silks, including parachute silk. In the next six pages, you will find dozens of examples of utility fabrics.

Light

Lighter-weight fabrics are brilliant for simple, filmy window treatments. Make decorative half-drapes from voile or gauze (see 24 and 27) panels with cased headings. Thread them onto narrow rods and anchor them within the window frame. Other lightweight drape ideas include unlined cotton (see 6, 7, 8) or linen (see 22) drops with tapes or ribbon loops at the top. Basic roller blinds in fine fabrics (see 9) look subtle and understated in a cream or white decoration scheme. Stiffening spray might be useful to give body to some gauzy fabrics. Perfect for bedrooms and bathrooms are filmy transparent loose covers in voile (see 12) for chairs with pretty, curvy shapes. Soft Indian cotton in bright lime green (see 26) and other hot up-to-the-minute shades are great for making up colorful and inexpensive throw-pillow covers. If you're in the mood, sew your own sheets, duvet covers and pillowcases in cotton sheeting (see 1), which comes in very wide widths. Covers should fit loosely around a duvet and have a generous opening secured with buttons, velcro, or simple ties to make them easy to slip on and off. Printed cotton lawn dress fabric is also worth considering for sprigged floral pillow-cases and throw-pillow covers. Cotton sheeting is also a great staple for lightweight tablecloths and napkins. I keep a huge length in white for parties indoors and out, when we have to fit lots of people around mismatched tables.

For full details of the fabrics shown on pages 38–43 see page 156.

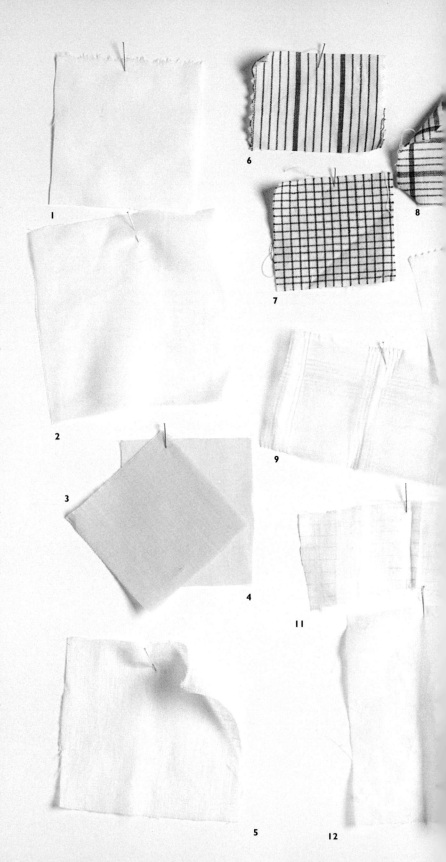

13

17

14

22

26

18

10

27

23

15

19

24

28

16

20

25

21

29

Versatile

I have a passion for blue-checked cotton (see 34 and 60) and use it all around the house for crisp color and detail, as throw pillows for assorted chairs (see 58 and 59), and as Roman drapes in dining and sitting rooms (see 34 and 59). Blue checked slipcovers also look good, and can be as basic or as decorative as you want—with bows, piping, ties, or button detailing, simple pleats, short skirts, or flowing hemlines. Window-seat pillows in cream linen with a piped trim are smart, and this also works well as an idea for covers on daybed bolster pillows. If the fabric is not shrink-resistant, and covers are to be washed rather than dry-cleaned, pre-wash all materials including piping before making, as different rates of shrinkage or bleeding can ruin the finished cover. Blue-and-white striped cotton, traditionally used for pillows and mattress covers, is also another favorite (see 45) and looks especially good as simple drapes with ties at my attic windows and across an alcove that houses children's clothes. Ticking—a robust cotton twill closely woven in narrow stripes—is also an attractive, classic idea for chairs and sofas. An all-time favorite is a lightweight, lavender-blue-and-white printed cotton (see 47) that I've used for tablecloths and chair covers for summer suppers out in the garden (see it made up as a loose slipcover on pages 120–21). Another discovery is woven cotton roller toweling bought from a company that supplies towels to hospitals and other institutions. Supplied on a seemingly endless roll, it makes simple and useful slipcovers (see pages 150–51).

54

47

48

42

49

43

44

45

46

50

51

52

53

55

56

57

58

59

60

61

62

63

64

65

66

67

Durable

Tough, all-purpose fabrics include canvas (see 82 and 83), sometimes known as duck, which is great for garden chairs and awnings. It's also good for Roman drapes, bolster covers, and as heavy-duty laundry bags (see pages 138–139). Cream-colored muslin is one of the best fabrics ever invented—it's incredibly cheap but manages to look smart and understated. It is also durable, washable, and perfectly practical. Muslin comes in a number of weights; the finer qualities are more appropriate for slipcovers or throw pillows, while thicker weights work well as insulating blinds (see 75), particularly if made in double thickness (see the Roman drapes project on pages 100–101), or for making drapes. Tough cotton denim (see 69) looks good on chairs after it's been put through several very hot washes to fade its dark indigo color. For a crisp, tailored look, or to show off techniques such as deep-buttoning, chairs demand tight coverings to emphasize their shape. A self-patterned, herb-green cotton and viscose with simple tulips is one of my favorite upholstery fabrics (see 87), and looks great on one of my secondhand armchairs. Sofas with a contemporary feel look wonderful in solid sea-green and blue colors in tightly woven cottons (see 88, 89, 90). Alternatively, plain cream cotton is stylish, but sensible for the dogless and childless only; choose some slightly more forgiving muddy-colored linen if you have a family to consider. Wool tartan (see 79) is another stylish idea for upholstering the seats of dining chairs or sofas, and it also works well as throws for keeping warm on long, cold, winter evenings.

78

82

83

87

93

79

84

88 89 90

94

80

85

91

95

81

86

92

96

Furniture

It may seem paradoxical, but I think that a diversity of objects can imbue an interior with a sense of character and uniformity. Old, new, decorative, industrial, contemporary, or utilitarian, it's possible to combine a variety of furniture styles under one roof and yet create a strong visual statement. Fashion pundits and supermodels dictate the length of hemlines from season to season, but thankfully, trends in interiors are less mercurial. Nevertheless, it is worth putting the same energies into assembling a look for your home as you would for your wardrobe. As with desirable outfits, buy your furniture only after considering texture, comfort, shape, and form. At home, I have gathered together items of furniture obtained from sales, second-hand stores, and family—everything from 18th-century oak dining chairs and old sofas to fold-up tables, painted junk filing cabinets, and kitchen chairs. My only proviso has been to weed out or revamp anything that I haven't liked the look of. Secondhand furniture designed for industrial use—such as metal swivel architects' chairs, library bookcases, and factory pattern-cutting tables—can be incorporated into your home. It can be better quality than its mass-produced equivalents.

Tables and Chairs

A fold-up slatted beechwood chair, ideal for storing away in small spaces, and an old wooden straight-back chair—excellent durable seating for kitchens and dining rooms.

Stackable contemporary seating with beech ply frame and splayed metal legs, inspired by the Fifties butterfly chair by Arne Jacobsen.

Sturdy shapes in solid wood: a rustic beechwood chair with rush seating and classic beechwood stool.

I like chairs without frills or gimmicky details, in other words, chairs that look good, are robustly constructed, and comfortable. Classic country chairs with rush seats are ideal for kitchens and dining rooms. Fold-up wooden-slatted seats—the staples of church halls the world over—can be stored away and are excellent for use in small spaces.

A crisp bright pink cotton slipcover and a touch of white paint have given an old chair a new lease on life.

A simple trestle table like this one in birchwood ply has a multitude of uses, ranging from a work desk to an impromtu dining table.

You can see examples of this Sixties-style weather-proof aluminum café chair in bars and cafés throughout Europe—a great idea for urban backyards and loft spaces.

Robust and utilitarian, a Swedish-style pine side table such as this could be used for displaying china, books, flowers, and other accessories.

Big and basic—a definitive kitchen shape in solid pine that can suit all kinds of interiors.

Essential folding shapes for indoors and out: a white slatted chair and a metal dining table.

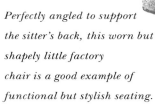

A white pickled paint effect is effective for sprucing up an old turn-of-the-century pine table like this one.

Customized with eggshell paint, this simple pine table would make a chic desk or sidetable anywhere in the house.

Like chairs, a table should look good, be strong, and a pleasure to sit at. A basic table top perched on trestles—probably one of the most useful and portable shapes—can be set up or collapsed instantly. Secondhand stores are always good sources for chairs and tables alike—take your pick and revamp worn pieces with a coat of paint.

Perfectly angled to support the sitter's back, this worn but shapely little factory chair is a good example of functional but stylish seating.

This crisp cotton checked cover with button detailing reinvents a basic muslin-covered dining room chair.

Based on a Fifties shape, a zinc-topped wooden table is a streamlined addition to a gleaming contemporary kitchen.

Beds

Beds should be chosen with practical and visual considerations in mind. To guarantee many peaceful nights of slumber, it is crucial at the outset of any bed-buying exercise to invest in a decent mattress and a solid base or frame. If you have limited funds, think about ways of revamping your existing bed. Lovely bedlinen and blankets can disguise even the ugliest studio-bed shapes.

right *A traditional cast-iron bed frame suits all kinds of interiors.*
below right *A Shaker-inspired pine four-poster (an amazingly good value assembly kit) is painted in white eggshell for a stylish understated finish.*
below *Spare in shape and detail and perfectly functional, this superbly streamlined bed in Douglas fir is a minimalist's dream.*

Sofas and Seating

Good springs and sound construction are essential for comfortable upholstered seating. It may be better to buy a good secondhand sofa or armchair with a wooden frame and strong interior springs, stuffing, and webbing than something new and less sturdy. Cover sofas with tough upholstery-weight linen or wool, or devise slipcovers which can be as basic as a throwover sheet or as tailored as a pull-on design in washable cotton.

top left *A Victorian Chesterfield sports decorative button detailing.*
left *This romantic French daybed is good for tight spaces.*
above *A contemporary shape, excellent for sprawling out on.*
right top *A Swedish-style wooden sofa with checked covers.*
right bottom *A generously proportioned and invitingly deep armchair.*

Cupboards and Storage

In an ideal world, storage should be designed to allow maximum living and breathing space. In reality we are hampered by budget, cramped rooms, too little time, too many occupants, and too much clutter to set about the task of arranging ourselves a little more efficiently. Here are some ideas to make clearing away a more fruitful and inspiring exercise. Basic wooden shelving is one of the cheapest means of storing everything, from kitchen paraphernalia to bathroom towels, or scores of books. Freestanding storage ideas include simple assembly-kit systems—these are basic structures in pine that are good for utility rooms and children's rooms. If home is an attic room with poor space, build assembly-kit storage systems or closets on site.

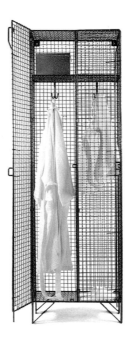

top left *Remember school lockers? This metal mesh closet is great for small spaces.*

top and far right *Inexpensively bought from secondhand stores, this filing cabinet and chest of drawers were improved by a fresh coat of paint*

right *Inexpensive but stylish assembly-kit cardboard drawers, designed for papers and home office work, are also ideal for storing odds and ends.*

far left *Laminated drawers with wire baskets are a clever idea for assembly kit kitchen units.*

left *In natural wood, a classic pine cupboard is a stylish kitchen staple.*

below left *Building a walk-in closet is one of the most effective ways of storing everything from clothes and trunks to suitcases.*

below *A decorative wooden cabinet or visellier like this looks at home in a country setting.*

Objects

If we each took an inventory of our possessions, how many things would we discover to be useless, or even something that we hated but couldn't give away because it was a present or a family heirloom? It might be painful for your conscience, but in the long run, paring down unnecessary household clutter eases the path to a more practical and soothing existence. Don't be sentimental about hoarding items that you will never use. Identify the things that give you pleasure to hold, to use, and to look at. It is more useful to have one superior saucepan than three second-rate ones that burn everything you cook in them. Even something as basic and utilitarian as a slender wood-and-bristle broom is a thing of beauty and just as humbly aesthetic as the rough mesh structure of a metal strainer or a good old-fashioned mixing bowl whose deep curvy proportions are perfectly evolved to perform its task. Do away with those dusty lamp bases made from Chianti bottles that your mother gave you for your first apartment. But resurrect classic Thirties-style gooseneck desk lamps, as those in the know continue to appreciate them. Vernacular objects perfectly designed to fulfill their function are works of art in their own right.

Utensils

Wooden cutting boards are kitchen staples, either for slicing vegetables or serving bread. Beechwood trivets protect kitchen surfaces from hot pans.

String is indispensable for everything from sealing jam pots to making an emergency clothesline. Keep a supply of wooden spoons for all mixing purposes. Use a spaghetti spoon to remove pasta from a pot.

A capacious flip-top stainless-steel trash can will handle large amounts of kitchen garbage, while a wood and bristle broom, found in any hardware store, is an essential tool for sweeping.

Whenever I have to make do with a temporary or makeshift kitchen during house renovations, the surrounding chaos is bearable as long as I have access to water, something to cook on (even if it's just a two-ringed portable stove), and a refrigerator. My survival kit of kitchen tools under such siege conditions includes a cast-iron enameled saucepan in which to

A glass juicer is a nifty tool for producing small amounts of orange, lemon, lime, or grapefruit juice.

Found in most continental kitchens a classic stove-top espresso maker, is an easy way to make ready supplies of steaming-hot strong coffee.

Life would be impossible without a good sharp stainless-steel knife, a pair of scissors, and a corkscrew!

Produce mounds of crisp, crunchy vegetables that really keep their flavor, or poach small pieces of fish, with a good heavy stainless-steel steamer.

A robust cast-iron enameled casserole is excellent whether you are cooking for a crowd of friends or just for one or two people, or preparing a simple family meal.

Drain everything from pasta and rice to salad greens with a metal colander, and borrow or buy a long fish steamer to take the angst out of cooking large fish like salmon in one piece.

For seafood: a strong oyster knife with a protective guard and classic flatware with bone-handled knives.

conjure up everything from break-fast-time oatmeal to herbed chicken casseroles; a sharp knife; a pile of wooden spoons; and, to keep the spirits from flagging and the caffeine levels high, a metal espresso maker that sits on the stove top. Other crucial equipment includes a garlic crusher, scissors, and of course, a decent corkscrew for opening wine.

Some of my favorite tools: a garlic crusher (that also stones olives), a balloon whisk, and lobster crackers, ideal for attacking crab.

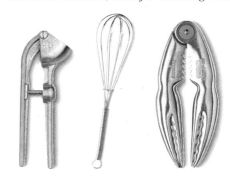

Some basic metal tools: a strainer for sifting flour or draining vegetables and a grater for demolishing hunks of cheese such as Parmesan.

What kitchen would be complete without a kettle? Invest in a sturdy and hard-wearing metal catering one for endless rounds of satisfying brew-ups.

Wonderful to hold and perfectly proportioned, a stainless-steel skillet for rustling up everything from risotto to fishsteaks.

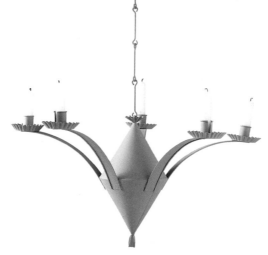

Lighting

We can appreciate that daylight is the perfect light, because there is the dark with which to compare it. But night suffuses everything with its own particular mood and bestows its own impressions and textures. Without darkness we would be deprived of the luxury of candlelight, which is the most sensual, calming, and benign of all sources of light. Lit candles highlight a dark room with a luminous quality that brings us in touch with the sensations of a pre-electric age. For a romantic dining room, invest in a simple metal or wooden chandelier, and light it with candles at every opportunity. At its best, artificial lighting is subtle and effective. At its worst, the glaring horrors of rooms with naked light bulbs or the bland brightness of supermarkets and airport waiting rooms speak for themselves. The most sensitive way to light interiors is with pools of subtle illumination, achieved with lamps set in corners or with low-voltage recessed lighting.

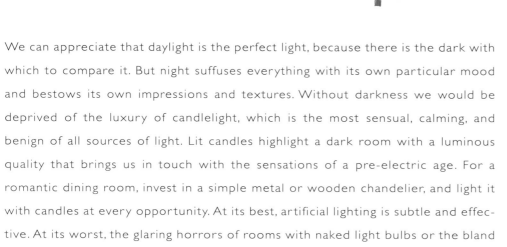

Different ideas for candle holders range from simple painted wood or metal chandeliers to pleated flameproof shades with brass suppports—as the candle burns the shade moves with it. For summer evenings, choose from curvy glass hurricane shades, lanterns, and nightlights (easily found in hardware stores).

Utilitarian lamps and
work lights look great in
contemporary and tradi-
tional settings alike.
Overhead pendant lights
in spun aluminum work
well in kitchens and din-
ing rooms, or as stylish
hall lights. For desk tops,
Thirties-style gooseneck
lamps are not only chic but
flexible practical gadgets
that help illuminate all
kinds of tasks.

57

Storage

Many small-scale storage ideas can be customized to look individual and imaginative. Reinvent old shoe boxes, for example, by covering them with fabric or paint to provide colorful storage for your home office or for children's toys. Or use a touch of white paint to transform an ugly black clothesrod into a stylish movable closet, ideal for small living spaces. It can be covered with a white sheet to repel dust. I am an avid collector of old jars and other household basics that double as stylish containers, including metal buckets (good for vegetables) and glass mason jars (they make staples like rice, flour, and pasta look good). Industrial meat hooks are available from good kitchen supply stores, and suspended from poles they are a great way to hang up your *batterie de cuisine.*

A wooden vegetable crate, procured from the local supermarket, is smartened up with lime-green paint and provides instant kitchen storage.

A thrift store basket is a useful solution for bulky items when they are not in use, such as this thick checked blanket made in Wales and a pair of bright green-and-blue cotton pillows.

Empty jars with neat good-looking proportions are ideal for accommodating anything from pens and pencils to flowers.

A simple pine chest has many uses, from organizing a messy desktop to housing fabric samples in a studio, or herbs and spices in the kitchen.

Empty wall space can be put to good use with a simple Shaker-style peg rack. These homemade drawstring bags are made from a washable blue-and-white checked cotton.

These Shaker-style boxes have been painted in one unifying color. Bright blue, used here, gives them a crisp clean look.

Mason storage jars are both utilitarian and stylish and can be filled with staples such as flour, sugar, cereal , and pasta.

A flat pine cabinet finished in latex is decorative and practical, displaying coffee cups, jars, and plates.

Hang meat hooks from poles for instant hanging space. This one is an old broom handle that has been painted and supported by metal hardware at each end.

An ugly black clothesrod has been transformed by a coat of white paint into a stylish and movable closet, ideal for small living spaces. It can be covered with a white sheet to repel dust.

Recycle old shoe boxes and cover them with bright cotton fabric as an attractive storage solution in the office, or for children's toys.

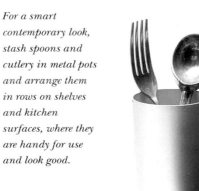

For a smart contemporary look, stash spoons and cutlery in metal pots and arrange them in rows on shelves and kitchen surfaces, where they are handy for use and look good.

A two-tiered wooden shoe rack, reminiscent of school locker rooms is useful for halls and bedrooms.

Display

above *Cheap wooden frames, painted in varying earthy shades and holding old postcards of beach scenes, look great arranged in compact rows on plain white walls.*
right *A favorite collection of old bowls is arranged simply in an old corner cupboard.*

Making a statement about the way you display favorite things, from photographs to kitchen pots and pans, is all part of creating an ordered environment and giving your living space a characteristic look. There is something arresting to the eye to see collections of basic vernacular objects—even plain white mugs can look good en masse.

Use natural elements to devise beautifully simple display ideas such as collections of pebbles from the beach; deep shadow boxes filled with leaves, shells, and china fragments from the shoreline; and bowls or jars planted with your favorite spring bulbs.

China and glass

Chunky white china mugs from just about any chain store are essential kitchen items.

Decorative designs for ceramics: blue-and-white tartanware for serving up shortbread, oatcakes, and other Scottish treats.

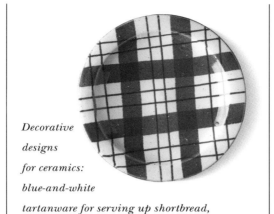

Any self-respecting café dispenses strong black espresso coffee in small heavy-bottomed cups with saucers. Imbibing out of anything larger, or flimsier would diminish the experience.

Blue-and-white striped china like this plate is bright, basic, and comes in lots of versatile shapes. It's great for everyday use.

The quality, shape, and size of what you drink out of or eat off is pivotal to relishing what is in your glass or on your plate. I like the ribbed, chunky qualities of Duralex glasses that are robust to drink from. The clean lines and classic proportions of plain white plates also make eating a pleasing affair for both the palate and the eye.

In contemporary sea-green, tableware that looks good in kitchens and dining rooms with green or cream schemes.

Glasses like this vibrant yellow one can inject bright color onto tables decorated in a clean white theme.

Workaday glassware for large drinks of cool iced water and other thirst quenchers or small glasses of sherry.

A choice of cups for dedicated coffee drinkers: tiny chocolate brown cups for small shots of caffeine, like rich dark mocha, or a heavy-bottomed cup for capuccino.

Jolly blue-and-white checked china is a cheery sight on the breakfast table. This shallow bowl is useful for dishing up cornflakes and other morning staples.

This classic jug shape has been around forever and comes in lots of different sizes. These jugs also make great vases for flowers.

Classic white bone china plates are my favorite and make the humblest meal look especially appetizing.

Blue-and-white spongeware is very decorative for informal settings, and it also looks good in hutches and on shelves.

You can't beat plain blue-and-white bone china for simple and stylish kitchen schemes—one of my all-time favorites.

Creamware looks brilliant in cream-painted country kitchens or dining rooms with decorating details in white and other neutrals.

Creamware china for refreshing brews, including a great big cup for warming milky breakfast coffees.

Perfectly formed bowl shapes—for serving everying from oatmeal and puddings to soups and salads.

PUTTING IT ALL

TOGETH

ER

Color and comfort are key ingredients in putting rooms together. Bright, light, airy shades of white and cream, as well as stronger greens, blues, and lavenders create inviting spaces. Choose furniture that combines function with style, and stick to basic shapes. To bring life into your surroundings, think about texture and draw inspiration from nature.

Culinary Living

An awesome number of items need to be squeezed into the average kitchen: boxes of breakfast cereals, pots, pans, dishwasher, refrigerator, sink—the list is endless. Storing and incorporating them all requires planning and thought. Cupboards, drawers, shelves, and work surfaces should be considered for both functional and aesthetic appeal. Make counters durable and use basic materials like wood, marble, slate, and stainless steel. Pare down your kitchen items to the most basic essentials. Make the daily ritual of eating as pleasurable as is practical. Eat from simple white plates, drink from good glasses, light candles, fill jars with flowers, and spread a crisp white linen cloth for special occasions. Preparing food can be a therapeutic experience even if you are busy with work or family. Avoid food fashions (what is it this month—French, Italian, or outer Mongolian?) and resist long drawn-out recipes with impossible-to-find ingredients. Don't become a nervous wreck looking for exactly the right

type of extra-virgin olive oil; if you can't find it, use what you already have. Stick to food that you like and can cook well. It is far better to serve up a simple but excellent cheese on toast than to produce an unremarkable attempt at something more flashy.

right *Wooden kitchen cupboards and drawers constructed from basic frames and painted in tough, matte creamy eggshell textures create understated and smart storage for kitchen items.*

In the past, kitchens were purely rooms in which to prepare and cook food, while dining rooms were dedicated to the pleasures of eating. To meet the demands of late 20th-century living, kitchens have evolved as spaces that fulfill many functions, so that eating and living are frequently combined. Different settings dictate different priorities. Rural kitchens need to cope with the to-ing and fro-ing of muddy feet or paws, and are the natural habitats of wonderful warming stoves such as Vikings, which are practical and stylish machines. In towns, there is more

emphasis on the clever placement of labor-saving devices such as the dishwasher, electric juicer, microwave, and so on, to help deal with the pressures of city life.

Most food preparation takes place on durable surfaces and there are various options. Oiled regularly and kept pristine with frequent scrubbing, a counter made of maple or beech is the ultimate luxury, albeit a costly one. A cheaper solution is to buy lengths of beech block from large hardware stores. Salvage yards are also a good source of reclaimed lumber for work surfaces; for example, I found a bargain teak draining board

from a Victorian almshouse at a country salvage yard. Despite its association with glossy Hollywood-style bathrooms, marble is a robust, hygienic material, and its unpolished, matte gray, white, or creamy textures make practical, understated work surfaces. Marble is particularly affordable at its source, namely in southern France, Spain, and Italy. For a really cheap kitchen facelift, laminated plywood is available in lengths from lumberyards and comes in many colors. The sink is a crucial part of the kitchen work surface, and deep-white ceramic sinks are ideal and can sometimes be picked up secondhand.

left *Clean uncluttered kitchens, with pots and pans stored on shelves or in cupboards, are places where you can set a big table and entertain your friends in style.*

Painted Storage Containers

Create stylish storage containers on a budget with utilitarian basics such as painted cans, vegetable crates, and terra-cotta flowerpots.

CANS MATERIALS

empty food cans

eggshell paint

1-inch paintbrush

CRATE MATERIALS

vegetable crates

eggshell paint

1-inch paint brush

FLOWERPOT MATERIALS

terra-cotta flowerpots

matte latex paint

1-inch paint brush

fine paint brush to apply design

pencil

small glass jars

CANS

Recycle used food cans—baked beans and tomato cans are ideal—by painting them to create smart storage containers for kitchen utensils.

INSTRUCTIONS

1. Carefully remove the lids, leaving a clean edge on the can and no lip.

2. Wash the empty cans in hot soapy water to remove the labels. If any glue remains, gently sand using a fine sandpaper. Sand the top rim to take off the sharp edge.

3. Apply two coats of eggshell paint to both inside and outside of cans.

CRATES

Obtain wooden vegetable crates from a local supermarket and jazz them up with paint to make great kitchen storage units. Paint them in various shades of country-kitchen cream, or be more inventive and experiment with bright blues, greens, and yellows, as shown here. As well as vegetable crates, you can adapt any kind of carton with a paint brush—I have made instant, colorful storage from shoe boxes and even breakfast cereal packets.

INSTRUCTIONS

1. Wipe down the vegetable crates with a damp cloth and sand lightly to remove any splintered wood. Pull out any nails that are sticking out and remove labels by scrubbing them with hot water or sanding them away.

2. Once the crates are dry and prepared, apply two coats of paint, sanding between coats.

FLOWERPOTS

Introduce splashes of color to a room with flower pots decorated in pinks, lavenders, or any other strong shade. Experiment with motifs—checks, stripes and scallops are just three to consider.

INSTRUCTIONS

1. Wash the flower pots, giving them a good scrub with a hard brush to remove all soil and dirt.

2. Place them in a warm place to dry out thoroughly. Any moisture left in the clay will stain the painted finish.

3. Apply two coats of white latex paint. When the paint is dry, take a pencil and lightly draw your design directly onto the pots.

4. Paint over the pencil lines in a contrasting color using the fine brush. Take care not to overload it with paint or you will have less control of your brush strokes. It is a good idea to blot the brush on some scrap paper first, to remove excess paint and to steady your hand. If any pencil lines still show when you have finished, remove them with a clean soft eraser after the paint has dried.

5. Flowers are kept in a jar of water inside the painted pot. The painted pots are not weatherproof and should not be left outside in rain.

left Open shelving, left as bare wood or painted in the same color as the rest of the kitchen, is a practical and decorative way to display china, kitchen cans, and containers.

Storage solutions are key to creating a well-organized kitchen. At the most basic level, simple open shelves in pine are incredibly useful for housing plates, glasses, culinary herbs, and just about any other kitchen paraphernalia. Collections of cans and boxes in interesting shapes and colors make an attractive display. Screw cup hooks to the underside of pine shelving and you have instant hanging space for mugs, ladles, strainers, and whisks. Not everyone is eager to have their kitchen contents on view, so cupboard doors hung on a basic frame are the perfect camouflage for canned goods or a repertoire of pots and pans.

Wall-to-wall units and cupboards are practical, but some custom-made schemes with fancy trims and detailing can be fantastically expensive. For a more individual look—and if you are strapped for cash anyway—combine a minimum of built-in elements such as a sink, stove, and counter in a unit, together with free-standing features such as a secondhand hutch jazzed up with paint, or an old metal factory trolley, which is ideal for wheeling plates and dishes around. Other

useful storage notions include a wall-mounted wooden plate drainer, or a tall, free-standing cupboard, ideal for filling with heavy items like food cans, groceries, and dishes.

right *A bright, cheerful kitchen with a utilitarian Forties feel. Pride of place is given to a magnificent Forties stove that cooks as efficiently as any contemporary model. Blue-and-white checked lino floor tiles and a crisp cotton tablecloth complete the homespun, relaxed atmosphere.*

top left *Practical and functional: a wonderfully deep granite double sink allows different washing tasks to be carried out at the same time, a great idea for large families or busy cooks who create a lot of washing.*

center left *Wooden shelving studded with cup hooks is a space-saving and attractive way of storing rows of smart blue-and-white mugs and basic drinking glasses.*

left *Although kitchen drawers are not an immediately obvious solution for storing china, in the absence of cupboards they work extemely well.*

right *In the streamlined and minimalist reinvention of a London terraced house, the area beneath the staircase has been artfully designed to contain storage behind a series of laminated flush-fitting cupboard doors.*

Kitchen surfaces with a smooth, streamlined, and contemporary edge are definitely no-go areas for clutter and chaos. Materials such as marble and zinc are practical counter ideas, while pans in durable stainless steel are good looking and functional.

left *Blue-and-white striped cotton roller toweling, used for chair covers or for table runners as here, can be obtained from specialty companies that supply institutions (see the project on pages 150–51 to make your own chair covers).*

below *Crisp plain white cotton tablecloths work in any setting. A row of narcissi planted in large basins creates colorful and scented decoration for parties and everyday settings alike.*

Eating and drinking, however humble and low-key an affair, should be reveled in and made the most of. Deciding what to eat at any particular meal, what to eat it on and what sort of mood you want to convey are of equal importance. At the end of a grueling day with three children, there are few frills at my table, but it's still worth lighting candles or finding some ironed linen napkins to create a sense of occasion. Table settings need not be elaborate affairs. Pleasing textures and well-made glass, china, and flatware are the crucial elements. On a day-to-day basis, you might settle for a crisp checked cloth with a jar of garden flowers, basic white plates, and simple glass tumblers. When friends come, it is worth making more of an effort and laying a crisp, white linen cloth and napkins, together with candles, your best bone-handled flatware and wine glasses. Sales are

good sources of discounted china and are where I go to buy seconds of white Wedgwood bone-china plates. Flea markets and thrift stores are useful for finding single pieces of antique glass. During a weekly hunt around my local market in London's East End, I pounced upon half a dozen late-Victorian heavy wine glasses, each one different, and use them to serve up everything from gelatin to drinks. Department stores, together with an ever-growing number of mail-order companies, are good sources of table linen. Alternatively, you could make your own tablecloths and napkins from special wide linen from fabric wholesalers, or sew fabric by the yard. If you're really stuck, simply use a plain white sheet. And if you have a children's party to organize, buy plain white disposable paper cloths, available from supermarkets.

One of the best things about assembling table settings is thinking of natural greenery and floral components for decoration. In the fall, plates of nuts or leaves look striking as do vases of branches studded with bright red berries. At Christmas time, I spray apples with gold paint and put them in' a big wooden bowl for a table decoration or hang them on string from a chandelier. I also scatter small branches of Christmas tree cuttings on the table, and for some early seasonal color and scent, I display pots of

Wooden dining chairs come in a variety of shapes. Don't worry if yours aren't all of the same design: a mix of styles, obtained from secondhand and thrift stores, can look just as good as a matching set.

above *Plain white china plates, bowls, and cups look great against any color scheme and they always make food look appealing, however humble it may be. Specialty catering stores can often yield good buys.*

flowering narcissi or hyacinths. In March and April I like to fill metal buckets with the bright green, sticky buds of chestnut branches or pussy willow, but summer tables are the most fun to create: I pick nasturtiums and sweet peas from my backyard and bring home armfuls of Queen Anne's lace after a day out in the country-side. Even a few jars of fresh herbs—rosemary, thyme, lavender, or parsley—make basic but beautiful decorations. Sometimes we've rented a cottage in the country, and there the summer hedges are thick with leggy purple foxgloves that make stunning table embellishments simply stuffed into tall, clear glass vases.

On trips to Spain, everyone eats out-side in the evening, sitting around trestle tables laid with grilled fish, meat, pasta, bread, wine, and cheese. After the glut of wild spring blooms such as orchids, daisies, buttercups, campion, and lilies, it's harder to find flowers during the months of summer drought. A useful source is the local farmer's market where Spanish ladies sell white tuberoses, a few stems of which produce a glorious, intoxicating scent as night falls. Otherwise, the table is decorated with vases of silvery gray olive cuttings. We get the barbeque going and cook up every-thing from sardines to slivers of bell pepper, zuccinni, and eggplant.

left Soft lilac paint on the walls is a good foil for covers in muslin and a plain white cloth. A lime-green checked cotton cur-tain and single stems of purple anemones provide a colorful contrast in this fresh and inviting dining set-up for two.

Making Preserves

These recipes, savory and sweet, have one thing in common: they are simple and satisfying to prepare, use fresh, natural ingredients, and are absolutely delicious. Choose from an aromatic pesto sauce for pasta, rich strawberry jelly, and deliciously smooth and sweet lemon curd.

STRAWBERRY JELLY INGREDIENTS

2 lbs strawberries, washed and
          patted dry, then hulled

2 lbs sugar with pectin

juice of a lemon

PESTO INGREDIENTS

2 oz basil leaves

2 oz pine nuts

3 garlic cloves

3 oz olive oil

2 oz grated Parmesan and

2 oz grated pecorino (or double the
amount of Parmesan)

LEMON CURD INGREDIENTS

grated rind and juice of 4 lemons

4 very fresh eggs

4 oz butter, cut into small pieces

12 oz sugar

STRAWBERRY JELLY

Wonderful just spread on toast with butter, strawberry jelly can be stirred into *fromage frais* for a simple pudding; layered between sponge cakes,

dolloped on scones

with cream, or used as a base for tarts and pies.

METHOD

1. Put all the ingredients in a preserving pan. Heat gently until the sugar dissolves, stirring frequently.

2. Bring to the boil and boil steadily for about 4 minutes or until setting point is reached. (A spoon-

ful on a cold plate will hold its shape, and when cool will wrinkle when pushed gently with a finger.)

3. Remove from the heat and skim off any scum with a metal slotted spoon. Let stand for 15–20 minutes to prevent the fruit from rising in the jars.

4. Stir the jam gently, then jar. Cover the jars with wax rounds, wax side down, then with cellophane rounds.

PESTO

Marked by the delicious herby and aromatic qualities of basil, this simple Italian sauce can be put together in a matter of minutes, and all of the ingredients are readily available from supermarkets. It is fabulous with pasta. Stir in 2 tablespoons for every serving and top with more grated Parmesan. Use it to accompany grilled swordfish or tuna steaks, or as a filling for baked potatoes.

METHOD

Place all the ingredients, except the cheeses in a food processor and whizz to a rough paste. Stir in the cheese. Serve immediately, or store in covered jars in the refrigerator and use within three days.

LEMON CURD

Making curd is one of the most delicious ways of preserving fruit. Limes and oranges both make very good curd, but the traditional favorite is lemon curd. Do not make huge quantities in any one batch as the mixture will heat through unevenly and be likely to curdle. Lemon curd is delicious by the spoonful straight from the pot. Less gluttonous suggestions include spreading it on bread, using it as pancake filling, lining the bases of fruit flans and pies, or making traditional individual lemon-curd tartlets. Also try serving it as a delectable dessert in tiny pots with homemade shortcake.

METHOD

1. Place all the ingredients in the top of a double boiler or a deep heatproof bowl standing over a pan of simmering water. (Do not allow the base of the bowl to touch the boiling water.)

2. Stir until all the sugar has dissolved and continue heating gently, without boiling, for about 20 minutes or until the curd is thick enough to coat the back of a wooden spoon.

3. Strain the curd into jars and cover with wax rounds, wax side down, then with cellophane rounds. Serve immediately or store it in the sealed jars in the refrigerator and use within three days.

Table embellishments can be very striking:
left *Topiary shapes work well in a terra-cotta flowerpot. Try a leggy myrtle standard, like the one shown here, or other tree shapes grown from plants such as box or bay.*
above *A pretty candelabra, a lucky find in a Roman market, looks especially lovely at night.*

The seating arrangement of any dining area depends upon space. If it is limited, tables and chairs might need to be of the fold-up variety and stored away if necessary. On the other hand, generously proportioned rooms can accommodate big wooden refectory tables, or oval and round shapes, and deep comfortable seating. Do not worry about having sets of matching chairs; disparate shapes, especially secondhand wooden kitchen chairs, can look quite good together, and if you want to create a sense of unity, you can cover them in simple pull-on slipcovers in muslin, woven cotton, or some other durable and washable texture. (See pages 78-79 for some colorful examples in blue-and-white striped roller-towel cotton, and the project on pages 150-51 for instructions on how to make your own.)

Choose a table to suit the style of the rest of the dining area. Rustic farmhouse shapes in wood look good almost anywhere and are practical and robust. Very contemporary streamlined models with zinc, stainless-steel, or laminated surfaces suit more modern settings. If furniture classics are your penchant, look to early 20th-century designs, such as the simple ladderback oak chairs and solid oak tables, or more recent classics such as the sensually molded, white bucket-shaped, Tulip chairs from the Fifties (see page 87). Since most people prefer brand new dining sets, excursions to flea markets and probing through secondhand stores can yield fantastic buys at bargain prices. If you need to create extra table space for a party, you can make a very basic dining table from a piece of board or even an old door laid over a pair of trestles. Simply disguise the makeshift base under a plain white sheet.

Other useful elements for dining areas include a side table or sideboard from which

left and above *Refectory style: a plain table and benches in solid Douglas fir pine is a spare and minimal solution for dining. Equally streamlined is the wall-length limestone bench seating and open fireplace.*

right *Low-backed wooden office chairs on wheels, and a mahogany door on metal trestles, are inventive ideas that are well suited to this contemporary living space in a London industrial building.*

to serve food or to display flowers or lighting. It's always handy to have a supply of plates, bowls, and glasses close at hand, either stored on open shelving or in cabinets.

One of the highlights of winter is enjoying an open fire. If you are lucky enough to have a working fireplace, gather some logs and kindling (or be practical and have them delivered!) and give your guests the luxury of a warming blaze. Candlelight is the best and most romantic light to eat by. I buy cream-colored church candles from a candlemaker at a nearby Greek Orthodox Church. If you don't possess particularly nice candlesticks, set the candles on plain white plates, or leave them free-standing for subtle illumination.

right *More colorful treatments for dining rooms include the yellow, green, and blue scheme here. Pale cream walls in eggshell paint create a plain backdrop for splashes of vibrant colors, as seen in these blue-and-white checked cotton Roman shades, sofa pillows in lime-green and blue, and a simple metal chandelier painted matte yellow. On the table, the plastic green checked cloth, available by the yard from department stores, is smart and practical for everyday use. The flowering spring bulbs were bought inexpensively by the tray from a local market and planted in painted flowerpots, to provide wonderful scent and sunny detail.*

Relaxed Living

Even the most frenetic workaholics need time to sink into comfortable chairs, put their feet up, and contemplate life. It's good to be nurtured by music, soft throw pillows, or a blazing fire. Living rooms are tailored to meet the demands of their occupants—families with small children require battleproof chairs and fabrics, while single individuals with no danger of sabotage by sticky hands might make a sumptuous wall-to-wall white scheme their priority. But whatever your family status, gender, or age, comfort and texture are the most important factors for the rooms in which you want to wind down. Use colors that soothe, and are light-enhancing—such as soft creams or bone whites—and keep paint textures matte. Buy solid, comfortable upholstery and proper, feather-filled throw pillows. Be selective with the fabric textures that you use. Seek out tough linens in beautiful creams and naturals or strong woven cottons in ticking, checked, and striped designs.

Experiment with bright plain colors such as blue, green, pink, and orange. Explore the variety of warm woolen fibers, for use as upholstery covers, soft throws, or insulating drapes. Be imaginative and buy yards of cheap gauze to make delicate drapes.

RELAXED LIVING

A living room should be a comfortable and relaxed area where you can sprawl out on a sofa with a good book, listen to music, watch television, or simply sit back and think. Color, comfort, texture, and warmth are important for putting together an agreeable, functional space.

From draperies to slipcovers, fabric colors can change a room as much as the impact of paint. Don't worry about slavishly matching the throw pillow to the curtain lining or the ties on your favorite slipcover. It is much more interesting to try similar but contrasting fabric shades. I remember a room I decorated in a spring theme where cream-yellow walls contrasted with bright green-

right *Blue-and-white is fresh used in decorative room details like crisp striped throw pillows and scrunchy Roman shades, faded floral covers, and checked cotton accessories.*

below *French metal daybeds look great with striped cotton ticking bolsters and plain white pillows or throws. Track them down at auctions or in antique shops and paint them white or leave them bare.*

Blues, greens, and grays are useful color tools.

left *Powder blue paint-work looks sharp against bold navy striped slip-covers, and pillows in assorted shades of blue cotton stripe. White brick-work walls and whitened parquet flooring emphasize the airy feel.*

far right *A painted gray baseboard adds subtle definition to plain white walls in a Provençal living room. Reclaimed terra-cotta tiles laid in an uneven pattern add to the vernacular effect.*

right *Warming not cold: rich blue-green paint makes a distinctive foil for white woodwork, a plain white dustsheet throw over an armchair and polished wooden floorboards.*

and-white checked blinds, together with slipcovers in a dark cabbage-leaf color and throw pillows in a lime-green and blue-and-white thinly-striped cotton. The effect was bright, sunny, and very easy to live with.

Living rooms must be comfort-able, and comfort relies partly on well-made and sturdy upholstery. It is more satisfactory to invest in a good-quality secondhand couch, say, than something that is brand new, mass-produced, and lightweight. I know an enterprising woman who sells every-thing from hand-me-down Knole sofas taken from mansions to junk armchairs, all to be found piled up in sheds at her farmhouse. If you invest in new upholstery, test it for comfort before buying: sit on it for ten

minutes, bounce up and down on the seat (you should be able to feel the underlying support); lean back (you should not feel any springs protrud-ing from the framework); lift it to test the weight of the framework (it should not be too lightweight).

Upholstery fabric should be hard-wearing. Some of the best fabrics are linen and linen-cotton mixes. A few years ago I found some wonderful earth-colored linen at a fabric outlet, on sale at fifteen percent off. I bought up ten yards which was enough to cover a Victorian chesterfield. Despite heavy wear and tear from parties, children, dogs, and cats, it still looks respectable, only of course I am now itching to find another bargain. Slip-covers are a practical way of cleaning and an economical way of updating sofas and chairs, and can be made

with various details such as pleated or simple box skirts, matching ties at the corners, or a row of buttons or a bow at the back. If you want an instant update, cover an unattractive sofa with a white sheet or a simple gingham-checked cotton throw. This is also a good idea for giving upholstery a change for the summer.

You can create a wonderful room with a great color scheme and lots of decorative ideas, but if it's cold, it's miserable. The ultimate in warmth and atmosphere is a blazing log fire—and woods such as chestnut and apple give off delicious smokey scents. Smokeless coal is an ecological second-best fuel. Not everyone has access to wood or the inclination to lay and maintain a real fire, so flame-effect fires are worth considering. Although they don't throw out as much heat as a real fire and can look artificial, they are not a bad compromise and many of the modern versions do a great job of fooling you into thinking they are real. Under-floor heating schemes involve hidden pipes connected to the central-heating system and are a great way of dispensing with unsightly radiators.

Splashes of terra cotta act as glowing detail in the cream-colored living room of a London Georgian townhouse. Among furnishing and fabrics in blues, greens, and yellows is a kelim rug in faded tones of earth and brick. Spread across the marble mantelpiece are old clay pots and a rosemary wreath. Other rich ingredients seen below include old wooden Spanish soup bowls filled with rag balls made of scraps of checked and striped cotton and an antique three-legged milking stool. Opposite, is a fold-up butler's tray with a candlestick lamp, and a jug of spring flowers.

Roman Shade

MATERIALS

muslin

batten, enough to fit the width of your
window

brackets

Velcro tape

staple gun or tacks

pins

needle

thread

sewing machine

looped shade tape

lath, 1½ inches wide

shade cord

screw eyes (as many as there are
rows of tape)

wall cleat with screws

A Roman shade is a simple and stylish window treatment for any room around the house and does not require massive amounts of fabric. For durability, make shades up in a tough fabric texture such as heavy canvas, linen, or muslin as in the creamy-colored example shown here, which has been self-lined to make it look smart from the outside.

TO MEASURE

1. Roman shades can either hang outside the window frame so that the entire frame is covered or, as illustrated here, they can fit neatly into a window jamb.

2. Measure the width and length of the window in order to calculate the amount of fabric you need. Cut two pieces of fabric each 3½ inches wider and 4½ inches longer than the window.

TO MAKE

1. To fit a Roman shade to the window it should be attached to a wooden batten, cut to fit the width of your window and hung from brackets fixed either side of the window frame.

2. I find it easier to take the shade down to clean it if it is secured to the batten by Velcro. Using either a staple gun or pin tacks, secure the toothed side of the Velcro to the uppermost edge of the batten.

3. Take the two pieces of fabric and, with right sides facing, pin, baste, and machine stitch them together along the two long edges and one of the short edges, using a seam allowance of ½ inch. Turn right side out through the open end and press all seams neatly.

4. Cut the ringed tape to the length of the shade. Pin the tapes down both sides 1 inch from the long sides and machine stitch in place through both

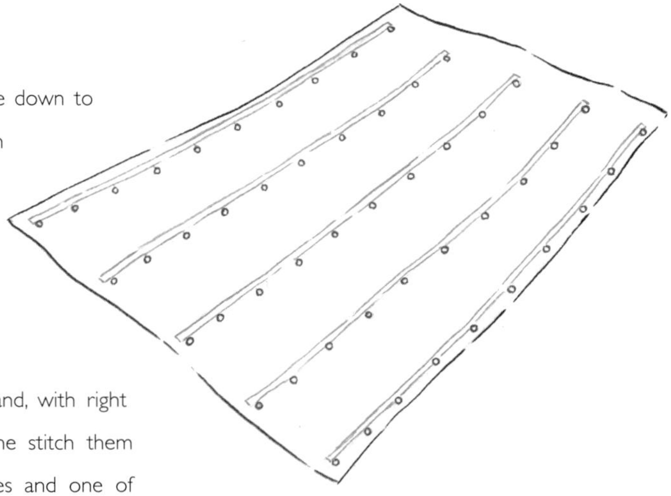

layers. Space the remaining tape evenly at approximately 12-inch intervals. Check that the loops on the tape are level across the shade, with the first row of loops 3 inches up from the open bottom edge.

5. To finish the bottom edge, turn under

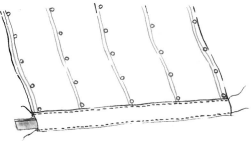

½ inch and then 1¾ inches, enclosing the ends of the tapes. Press and machine stitch along the hem, then make a row of stitching close to the folded edge. Insert the lath into the casing to stiffen the blind and to help it to hang well. Secure the ends with hand stitching.

6. Pin, baste, and machine stitch the other Velcro strip along the top back edge of the shade.

7. To calculate the amount of cord you need for each row of tape, measure twice the length of the finished blind plus one width. Tie a length of cord to each bottom ring and thread up through every loop in the tape.

8. Fix an eyelet into the lower edge of the batten above each row of tape. Attach the shade to the

batten, Velcro surface to Velcro surface, and run the length of cord through the eyelets, threading from right to left so that they all meet at the far left. Trim the cords to the same length and knot.

9. Fit the batten onto the window brackets.

10. Screw a cleat into the window frame so the cords can be secured when the blind is pulled up.

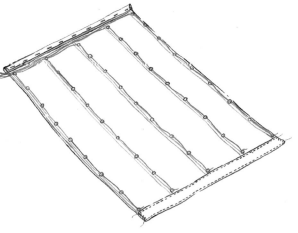

this page *Neutral tones of white and cream create a peaceful feeling. Contemporary details include market finds such as a Sixties basket chair, and sunburst mirror, together with simple picture frames and streamlined lighting.*

far right *Harking back to Fifties gum commercials, the owner of this cozy* *paneled living room in a traditional shingled house on Long Island aptly describes the subtle paintwork as chewing-gum gray. Rough sisal matting, pine planking (resourcefully salvaged from packing crates), and neutral-colored linen add to the fresh and understated effect.*

Pillows are always important comfort factors. Buy proper feather or kapok-filled pads; foam fillings are unsightly and lumpy. Pillow forms squeezed into stingy covers don't look good, so make covers roomy and allow the pillow to "breathe." Simple piped throw pillows or flanged shapes are perennial classics. Bags with tie openings look good and are incredibly easy to sew at home. You can make pillows out of just about any fabric—I like tough blue-and-white checked Indian cotton, striped ticking, and light cotton in bright shades (which is good for a summery feel). You can also sew new covers by using the material from old curtains, tablecloths, and scraps of fabric in your favorite colors or patterns. Anything faded and floral, especially blues and whites or soft pinks and lavenders will work well with checks, stripes, and solids. If, say, you hanker after a beautiful floral cotton but can't afford the hefty price tag for a big furnishing project, why not buy just half a yard—the same cost as the average price of a pair of shoes—and make it into a beautiful throw pillow cover for a favorite chair. It will last considerably longer than the shoes!

Deep-pile, wall-to-wall white carpet might be appropriate in a boudoir-like bedroom, but for stylish, everyday living, natural flooring textures such as coir, sisal, seagrass, and cotton or wool rugs in checks and stripes are more liveable with in terms of cost and practicality. For insulation, lay rugs over one another. Buy mats that are bound with burlap or woven cotton borders as they look better and don't fray. Cotton rugs are cheap, and many are designed to be thrown in the washing machine, but remember that very bright colors might run, so they should be carefully handwashed. Thick tartan-plaid wool rugs are a good investment.

far left *For a homespun feel with an updated edge, this loft space has been decorated with pristine white walls, galvanized metal buckets, and a primitive-style metal chandelier. Woven checked cotton bought in a sale has been used to make simple slipcovers for a battered old couch and chairs.*
left *More homespun ideas: disparate furniture from a sale is unified with soft gray paint.*

Slipcover for a Sofa

If you have an old sofa at home that is looking a bit worse for wear, do not get rid of it. An old sofa is usually far more solidly built than a new one, so it's worth giving it a fresh start. Complete re-upholstering can be very expensive, but this idea is simple.

MATERIALS

10 yards pre-washed white cotton drill, 60 inches wide

pins

tape measure

tailor's chalk

ruler

sewing machine

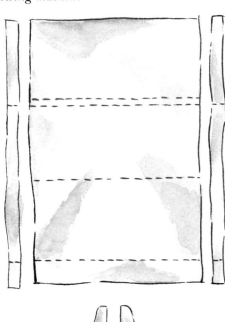

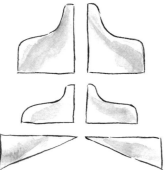

CUTTING AND MARKING THE FABRIC

1. Remove the cushions and mark a line down the center of the sofa with pins, front and back as shown. Measure the total distance and add 3 inches for hems; cut a piece of fabric to this length for the all-in-one back, seat, and front piece.

2. Fold the fabric in half lengthwise, with right sides together, and mark the fold line with tailor's chalk. Place this fold along the pinned center line on the sofa, letting 1½ inches hang down below at both the front and the back. Open out the cloth and smooth it into place to cover the sofa, pushing it tightly into the corners. Pin it to the sofa along the existing seam lines on the original slipcover.

3. On this sofa, a 3½-inch-wide band runs up and over the arm and down the back of each side. To cut out the correct amount of fabric for these bands, measure this total length and add 3 inches for hems. The width should be 5 inches. Pin the strips onto the sofa arms and down the back along the side seam lines, allowing a 1½-inch seam allowance to hang down at both the front and the back. Using your chalk, mark a line where the front and the top of the back sections of the sofa meet the bands. This will be your reference for matching up the pieces when you are making the cover.

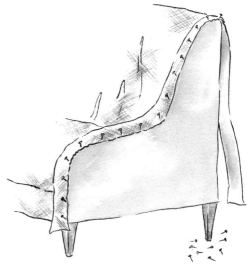

4. To cut the outside arm pieces, fold the fabric in half and hold it against the side of the sofa, making sure the straight grain is vertical. Cut out the rough shape of the arm leaving a good 3-inch seam allowance. Using the same method cut the inside arm shapes. Pin all four pieces, right side down, onto the sofa along the seam lines.

5. In between the side back and the back strip is a triangular gusset which allows the cover to slip easily on and off.

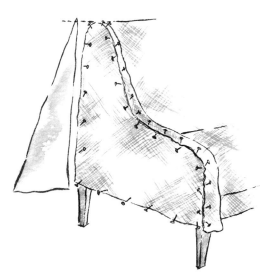

Cut out two triangular pieces of material. Each one should be 10 inches at the widest point across the bottom. The height of the triangles should be equal to the height of the sofa back, plus ¾ inch for the top seam allowance and 1½ inches for the bottom hem. Join up these two points to form the third sides of the triangles.

Mark three equidistant points down each side of the gussets for the ties. Set them aside.

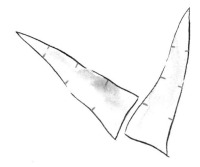

6. Mark the position of the seams with tailor's chalk on all the sections following the pinned lines. Mark the junctions clearly with corresponding numbers so you know exactly which sections must be sewn together. Carefully remove the fabric and straighten the drawn seam lines with a ruler. Trim off all excess fabric leaving a uniform ¾-inch seam allowance.

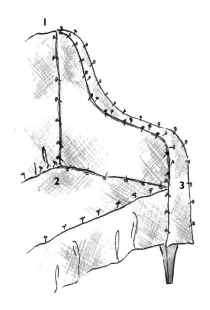

HOW TO MAKE THE COVER

I. To make the gusset ties, cut two strips measuring 40 × 1½ inches. Divide each strip into six sections and cut again. For each tie, turn under ¼ inch along both the long and one short raw edge and press. Fold the ties in half lengthwise, wrong sides together, and machine stitch along the folded edges.

2. Attach the ties to the wrong side of the gusset, at the points marked previously, by machine stitching across their width.

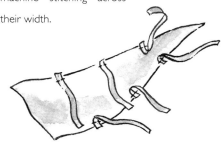

3. With right sides together, machine stitch both inside arms to the sofa seat back and the seat.

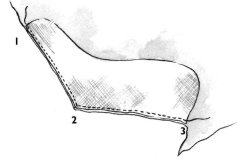

4. Machine stitch the bands to the inside arms and the main cover, right sides together, matching the marked seam lines and numbers.

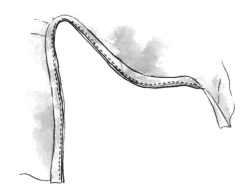

5. Next, attach the outside arm sections to the band, with right sides facing, matching the seam lines and the corresponding numbers. Machine stitch the pieces together along the arm seam, but leave the back section open so that the gusset can be inserted.

At this stage, your sofa cover should look like this. The shape is now recognizable, but the back is still loose, as the side gussets and ties are yet to be inserted.

6. Insert the gusset between the outside arm piece and the back section of the band. With right sides together stitch them in place.

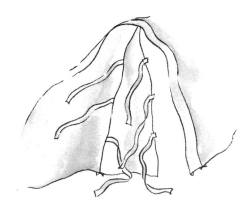

7. At this stage, place the cover on the sofa to check the fit and length. The gusset will allow for a certain amount of flexibility so make any adjustments if necessary. Remove the cover and trim the seam allowances. Hem the bottom by turning under ¼ inch followed by a further ½ inch, and then stitching all round.

TO MAKE THE CUSHIONS

1. To make two 27½ × 24½ × 4-inch cushions, cut four rectangles, each measuring 29 × 26 inches for the seat.

2. For the sides, cut two strips of fabric measuring 78 × 5 inches and for the backs cut two strips 29 × 7 inches, each of which must then be cut in half along the length.

3. Make up some ties as for the gusset. Allow six for each cushion and mark their position on the opening edges of the back sections. Press under ¼ inch, followed by ½ inch along these edges. Place the short raw edge of the ties under this turning and stitch along the length of the back opening through all layers, keeping close to the edge.

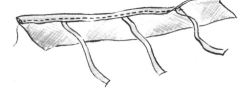

4. For each cushion, place the two back pieces together with the seamed edges meeting. With right sides together, stitch the side strip to both ends of the back section, using a seam allowance of ½ inch.

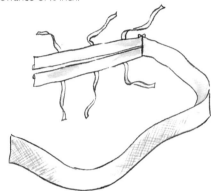

5. Mark the corner positions on each strip and turn them wrong side out; line up the top and bottom seat rectangles with these marks. Pin, baste, and machine stitch them in place with right sides together, using a ½-inch seam allowance.

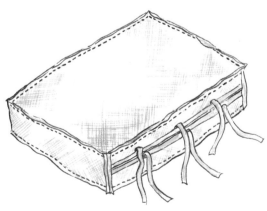

6. Trim the corners, turn the covers out, pull through the ties, and insert the cushion pads.

Textures help determine the style and look of a room. Country-cottage living rooms need rustic injections of rough wool throws, wood floors, tough sisal mats, and hand-woven log baskets. Streamlined contemporary settings need smooth touches such as slipcovers in crisp white cotton which help unify mismatched chairs and complement pale wood floors. Modern materials such as zinc and aluminum for lighting and table surfaces also emphasize a more up-to-date look.

Curtains and drapes take substantial amounts of fabric, but need not break the bank. Stick to simple headings such as loops and ties. Choose strong cottons and linens. If you buy ten yards or more from fabric wholesalers, many will

left *Comfortable yet functional living spaces with seating covered in robust ticking or muslin.*
below *A small space set aside for a home study area successfully houses vital office elements, including a basic trestle table, a metal filing cabinet, cardboard box files revamped with paint, and a smart metal Twenties-style desk lamp.*

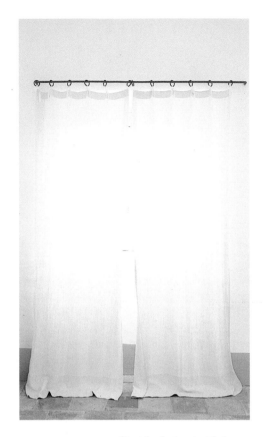

right Fresh and filmy: soft cream-colored linen drapes with a decorative double-layered heading, recycled by the owner from a previous apartment. An extra-long painted wooden pole and rings create a unifying effect.

Simple shapes in plain fabrics create light and airy window treatments:
above *Light cotton curtains draped to the floor. They are simply tied onto a metal pole, bought by the length and bent over at the ends.*
right *Heavy canvas with eyelets can be hooked onto a window frame and pulled back as required.*

give you a substantial discount. Line curtains for a better "hang" and also to protect them against fading due to sunlight. Interlinings give greater insulation; bump is the thickest and looks like a blanket, while domette is a brushed cotton and the most commonly used. Roman or plain windowshades are useful for providing extra insulation with curtains, as well as protecting from the sun (see the project on pages 100–101). Shades also suit just about any window shape. I like Roman shades and I have examples in checked cotton and plain muslin hanging at my Georgian windows; these are all hand washable in the bath. Unlined curtains in filmy textures such as voile and organdy are cheap, stylish options. If you live in a climate with hot summers and cold winters, have two sets of curtains, light ones for the summer and warmer pairs of thermal ones for the winter. Paint curtain poles the same color as walls for a unifying effect. Inexpensive ideas for poles include wooden doweling from lumberyards cut to length and painted, and stretchy wire available from hardware stores that is ideal for small drops, for example, in cottage windows.

Potpourris

The wood shavings and dried flowers in many shop-bought potpourris are no match for the simple scented examples you can make yourself. It is easy to dry garden flower petals, herbs, and citrus fruit slices and peels. For scent, use drops of deliciously fragrant essential oils and enhance the aroma with a fixative such as orris root powder or cloves. Alternatively, buy ready-made oil blends from herbal and potpourri specialists or read books on the subject to create your own subtle tailor-made examples.

MATERIALS

china bowl for mixing
seal or lid for bowl
wooden spoon

SUMMER FLOWER POTPOURRI INGREDIENTS

4 oz lavender flowers and stems, pinks flower heads, delphinium petals, rose petals, hydrangea petals, and any other flower petals
½ oz orris root powder
20 drops geranium oil

HERBAL POTPOURRI INGREDIENTS

2 oz bay leaves
2 oz rosemary cut into 6-inch lengths
½ oz whole cloves
20 drops rosemary oil

ORANGE AND LEMON POTPOURRI INGREDIENTS

1 lb oranges
½ lb lemons
8 whole clementines
25 drops orange oil

SUMMER FLOWER POTPOURRI

My mother makes this with as many petals and flower heads as she can collect from her garden in the summer. The faded colors give it an old-fashioned country garden effect.

INSTRUCTIONS

1. Dry the flowers on sheets of paper in an airing cupboard or similar warm dry space.

2. Using the wooden spoon, mix the dried flowers and orris root powder in a bowl. Take care not to damage the flowers. Add the oil and mix again. Seal the bowl for four weeks to allow the fragrances to develop and then transfer the potpourri to your favorite dishes and containers.

HERBAL POTPOURRI

I like the muted greens of this aromatic mixture. It looks lovely in white bowls on a sideboard or kitchen hutch. Even dried, the bay leaves retain a little of their fresh scent, and the herbal effect is enhanced with the addition of rosemary oil.

INSTRUCTIONS

1. Dry the herbs on a sheet of newspaper in an airing cupboard or similar warm, dry space.

2. Using the wooden spoon mix the herbs in the bowl. Add the rosemary oil and then mix again. Seal the bowl for at least four weeks to allow the oil to work and then transfer to your chosen containers.

ORANGE AND LEMON POTPOURRI

Slices of dried citrus fruits scented with orange oil look and smell earthy and organic.

INSTRUCTIONS

1. Remove the peel from the oranges and lemons, taking care to leave the pith behind and then slice the fruit into thin rounds. Retain the peel. Make incisions in the clementines, making sure that the whole fruit remains intact. Lay everything to dry on a sheet of newspaper in an airing cupboard or warm place.

2. When dry, transfer the fruit into a bowl and mix with a wooden spoon. Add the orange oil. Mix again. Seal the bowl for four weeks and then transfer to individual containers; shallow bowls are best because the slices can then be arranged in layers.

Sleeping in Style

We do so much of it that sleep deserves to be a peaceful and luxuriating experience. On a cold winter's night, it is bliss to curl up in crisp white bedlinen and warm wooly blankets. Conversely, in summer it's good to lie with the sparest of bedclothes, say just a fine cotton sheet and an open window to catch a cooling nighttime breeze. Bedrooms need to be quiet airy refuges away from domestic distractions. There should be lots of cupboards, boxes, or ample closet space to store clothing and clutter. Some of the best ideas include spacious built-in, walk-in closets with simple paneled doors. Old laundry baskets, big wooden boxes, and even old shoe boxes covered in fabric and paint are also useful bedroom storage notions. Bedroom textures need to be soft and inviting, such as gauze curtains, plain muslin blinds, fine cotton pajamas, and fluffy toweling robes. Soft wool checked blankets in cream or blue are great for dressing beds. Then there are antique quilts, with pretty floral designs, that look lovely folded or draped over a bedstead. Spend as much as you can afford on bedding—soft goosedown duvets and pillows are the ultimate bedtime luxury. It is also prudent to invest in a strong mattress that does not sag and bend.

A bedroom is a sanctuary, away from work and other people. It is a place where you can curl up between crisp sheets with a good book to read, a hot drink, and a bar of chocolate. Asleep or not, all of us spend so much time there that it should be the one room in the house where we can be indulgent. Bedroom textures should be luxurious, soft, and warm. The stresses of the day fall away when you climb into white cotton sheets, curl up under soft blankets, and warm yourself up in cold weather. It pays to invest in the best bedding you can afford and to take time in choosing the right bed.

There are all sorts of bed shapes to suit the look you want to achieve. At a basic level, there is a studio bed which can be dressed quite simply. It is useful in a bedroom that doubles as a daytime living room or study.

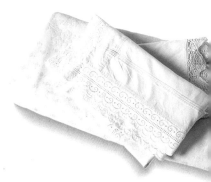

Comfort factors in bedrooms include freshly laundered sheets and warm cream-colored wool blankets. Search markets and secondhand stores for old bedlinen; the quality is often better than modern textures. Worth looking out for are old damask bedcovers and fine embroidered linen pillow cases. Sleep peacefully in a traditional bedstead: classic brass always looks wonderful and decorative ironwork looks great painted white. Create a calm oasis by keeping the room clutter free.

MATERIALS

metal chair
tape measure
pattern paper
pencil and pen
pins
scissors
striped cotton
needle
thread
sewing machine

Slipcover for a Metal Chair

A simple metal chair can be totally transformed with a coat of cheerful white paint and a tied slipcover. Here, fresh blue-and-white striped washable cotton is tailored to the shape of the chair so that it retains its gently curved outline. You can remove the cover for washing and slip it off after use.

INSTRUCTIONS

1. First measure up the three parts of the chair to be covered: the seat (A), the inside back (B), and the outside back (C). Transfer the dimensions of A, B, and C onto pattern paper, adding a ½-inch seam allowance all around. For the outside back panel (C), cut the paper pattern in half vertically, splitting it into two parts, and add a ½ inch seam allowance to both straight edges. This will form an opening at the back of the chair so that the cover can be easily slipped on and also removed. Cut out all four pieces in the striped cotton fabric, but make sure that the direction of the stripes remains consistent (see below). On piece A mark the positions of the two rear chair legs with a cross.

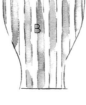

2. To make the frill, measure around the edge of the front of the chair seat from one rear leg to the other. Then multiply this measurement by three.

3. Cut out a strip of fabric 6 inches wide and stitch together strips to the required length, measured in the previous step. Turn under the bottom edge and sides of the strip. Pin, baste, and machine stitch, leaving the top edge for gathering. With contrasting thread make gathers along the top edge so that the frill fits the perimeter of the front of the seat.

4. When the strip is fully gathered, align the arrow marked above with the arrow marked on pattern A. Pin, baste, and machine stitch the gathered frill to the front perimeter of piece A, with right sides facing, stitching inside the line of gathering stitches.

5. To make the ties, cut two strips of fabric, each 1 inch wide and 6¾ inches long. Fold in half lengthwise, right sides facing, and machine stitch along a short and a long edge. Turn right side out and hand sew the open end closed. The finished tie should be ½ inch wide. Repeat for the second tie and press. In the same manner make two shorter ties 1 inch wide.

6. Position the longer ties centrally over the crosses marked on piece A, indicating the position of the rear chair legs. Sew firmly in place (see below).

7 Place two halves of C right sides together. Stitch one third of the way along, forming a central seam. Turn in, pin, and hand sew the remaining raw edges (see left). Place pieces B and C right sides together. Pin, baste, and machine stitch along both the sides and the top. Turn right side out.

8. To complete the frill, cut out a strip 6 inches wide and three times length of the seat edge between the two rear legs. Cut the strip in half to make the opening. Turn under the bottom and side edges. Pin and machine stitch, leaving the top edges for gathering.

9. Stitch the gathered, frills right sides together, to the bottom edges of piece C. Attach the remaining ties to the rear opening to fasten.

10. Pin, baste, and machine stitch the bottom edge of panel B to the back edge of piece A, right sides together. Press. Slip over the chair and fasten the ties.

below *Gray paintwork and a simple painted bedside table, together with a subtlely checked blue wool blanket and a glass of vibrant yellow spring daffodils, inject color into the overall neutral effect created by the white walls and bedlinen in this Provençal farmhouse bedroom.*

right *Brilliant blues lend a seaside air to a Long Island bedroom. Blue-and-white patchwork quilts and boldly striped cotton pillowcases add to the bright and breezy feel, while a faded denim child's sailor suit on the wall brings a jaunty touch to the coastal theme.*

I prefer bright and airy bedrooms in whites and creams—in other words, rooms that have a light ambience throughout the year. Darker, richer colors such as library green or study red may suit some individuals, but waking up to moody walls on dark mornings during a long winter may quickly become a gloomy prospect. Bedrooms need to be comfortable, optimistic places, with supplies of good reading matter, soft bedside lighting, some sort of seating, and maybe a bowl of favorite, scented flowers.

There is nothing to beat the simplicity of plain white bedlinen. It is smart, stylish, and unassuming. When an injection of color is desired, you can look to bold, contemporary designs, perhaps in tomato red, lime green, fuchsia pink, or lemon yellow. Bedlinens in such colors work particularly well in southern climates with strong light. It seems that country style with its fussy floral-patterned sheets and pillowcases has had its day on the decoration scene (and none too soon). But for the mass market, manufacturers persist in launching frilly, flowery designs that make beds look like the tops of chocolate boxes. However, florals in the bedroom can look really pretty if used carefully and with restraint. Take for example, a simple lavender-colored country bedroom theme, suitable for a cottage bedroom. You can make basic pillowcases in a delicate rosebud print (note that dress fabrics often have more subtle floral designs than their furnishing counterparts) and combine them with white sheets and pillowcases, and a faded antique floral patchwork quilt. Stick to a plain cotton window treatment, paint the walls white, and cover the floors in cheap, neutral cotton rugs. The whole effect is stylish and not in the least bit overdone or too pretty.

left *A romantic mahogany* bateau lit *is a great vehicle for layer upon layer of wonderful white antique bedlinen. A filmy mosquito net, functional as well as decorative, is generously swathed from the ceiling to complete the translucent effect.*

right *Distinctive in texture and color, smooth polished parquet flooring and bentwood furniture provide smart, dark contrasts to creamy walls and bedlinen in a Parisian apartment.*

Forced to make up my own bed from an early age, I think that an orderly, uncluttered bedroom helps to set you up mentally for whatever difficulties and chaos you may come across during the day. Storage, of course, is a key issue. It is quite surprising how a few pieces of casually flung clothing or perhaps a modest pile of discarded newspapers create a bedroom scene that begins to look like a rummage sale. Built-in shelves with doors along one wall are a very successful way of storing clothes, hats, shoes, bags, suitcases, and other closet necessities. Free-standing armoires and chests are useful, but impractical if space is tight. If you are restricted to a budget, you can always curtain an alcove with muslin, linen, or even an old bedspread. Except for a couple of hours spent at the sewing machine, the results are almost instantaneous and

very stylish. A large chest of drawers is always useful for swallowing up smaller items of clothing and spare bedlinen. Old trunks, big boxy laundry baskets, and modern-looking zinc boxes are also useful bedroom storage devices.

Bedsteads offer a variety of decorative possibilities. A Shaker-style painted wooden four-poster frame looks good with tie-on curtains, a muslin or linen valance, or left entirely bare. Good-value examples are available in assembly kit form, nineteenth-century French metal daybeds are excellent for dual-purpose rooms and look really smart with ticking bolsters and pillows; they are not difficult to find if you track down dealers who specialize in antique French decorative furniture. If there are children in the family, consider bunk beds. Available in most department stores or large furniture warehouses, they are a very good value and can be dressed up with a coat of paint.

Those of us who enjoy the pleasures of a firm bed know that high-quality bedding really does help toward getting a good night's sleep. The best type of mattress is sewn to size with layers of white curled hair, together with fleece wool

left A country feel is evoked by matte painted paneling, a green wooden bed, and simple fabrics and furnishings in a Georgian townhouse. An antique lavender-colored patchwork quilt with a seaweed design and pink floral sprigged pillowcases made up in lawn dress fabric provide colorful and fresh detail.

left *Hot shots: vivid splashes of bright color work well in sunny southern climates. Experiment with cool cotton bedlinen in bold blue, green, yellow, pink, and orange. As temperatures soar, practical ideas for keeping cool are essential: windows flung wide open let air flow through, light gauze curtains help catch a breeze, and stone flagstones stay cool underfoot.*

and white cotton felt, all incorporated with solid box springs. Perfect pillows are combinations of duck down and feather, gray duck feather, or the ultimate luxury, white goose feather. And for people with allergies there are special hog and cattle hair versions available. It is worth your while spending a little bit more when it comes to buying bedding, both for increased comfort and longevity.

My dream is to sleep in linen sheets that are laundered and pressed daily. Until this fantasy is realized, I shall be content with a box of assorted cotton linens at various stages of wear and tear. My softest sheets are Egyptian cotton, bought years ago and still going strong. I also love antique bedlinen and have various Victorian linen and cotton lace pillowcases, as well as the odd linen sheet handed down from elderly relatives or bought in thrift stores and flea markets. Although pure linen sheets are very costly and need extra care and maintenance, they will last a lifetime. Secondhand linen should be clean and starched, and feel crisp and tightly woven. Modern linens shed creases faster than traditional ones, reducing the need for ironing.

Duvets have become an almost universal item of bedding, but sheets and blankets are still popular. The practical thing about layers of bedclothes is that you can simply peel back or pull on the layers to suit the temperature. In spring, for example, a cotton blanket and sheet may be all that is necessary and, when the air conditioning is on in midsummer, nothing beats the addition of a wool blanket with a satin ribbon binding.

below *Bunk beds are an economical and useful idea for children's bedrooms; they are space-saving as well as fun to sleep in. Update and give a stylish look to a plain pine bunk bed by painting it with a coat of pale eggshell paint, as seen here.*

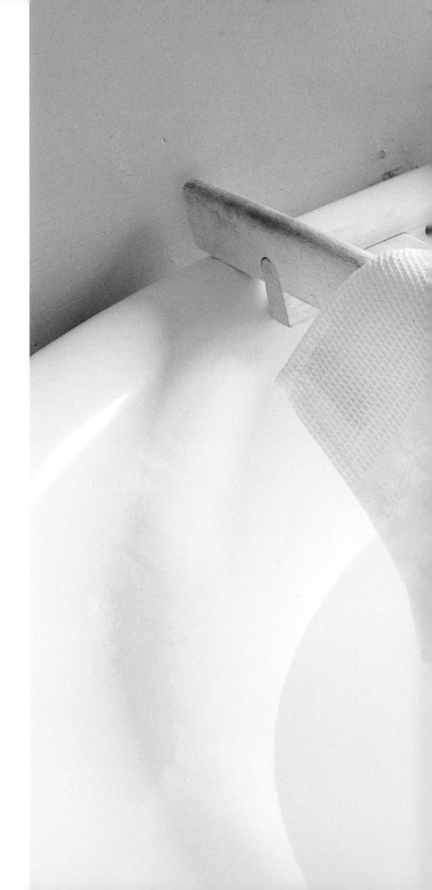

Clean Living

To start the day, an invigorating shower, or simply a wash in a basin of hot water, wakes you up and triggers circulation. At other times, and especially at the end of the day, I can spend hours soaking in a tub of steaming hot water, listening to the radio (sneaking off for a mid-afternoon session is also highly recommended for a rare treat). They may not be the best at conserving heat, but smooth cast-iron baths are definitely the most agreeable to soak in. It's good to scent the water with fragrant oil or work up a creamy lather with soap. A bleached wooden bathrack is a useful vehicle for storing soaps and washcloths and keeping reading material dry and within reach. Loofahs, sponges, and brushes are also essential bathroom tools for keeping skin pristine and well scrubbed. To accompany daily washing rituals, use fluffy cotton towels in white, seaside blues, and bright spring-green colors. Bathrobes in toweling or soft waffle cotton are also delicious ways of drying off—buy big

sizes for really wrapping up well. The best showers soak you with a powerful delivery of water, and have finely tuned faucets that deliver hot or cold water as you require it. Invest in duckboards and soft cotton bathmats to mop up the inevitable pools of water.

A bath, a shower, or even a quick face splash are instant revivers and help relieve the stresses of daily living. Like eating, washing can be a deliciously sensual ritual. It can vary from a short, sharp, invigorating cold outdoor shower on a hot summer's day to a more languid experience in midwinter when a long, hot, steaming bath is the perfect antidote to dark days and icy temperatures. Copious supplies of hot water are at the top of my list of crucial bathroom ingredients—even the meanest, drab, and cramped little bathroom can be acceptable if it delivers piping-hot water, and plenty of it. Scented soaps and lotions are essential elements too. Among my favorites are delicately scented rosewater soap and rose geranium bath gel. If I'm in the mood for more pungent aromas, I choose stronger scented spicy soaps with warming tones.

White bathrooms are bright, light, and airy, as shown by the gleaming examples pictured here. Walls and woodwork are finished in varying shades of white and are complimented by pristine ceramic tiles, baths, and sinks. Deliciously tactile textures include big fluffy towels, soft sponges, and tough cottons for laundry bags.

Bathroom Wall Cabinet

Give a basic pine bathroom cabinet a new look with seaside-inspired green-blue paint, and a utilitarian but stylish chicken-wire front. You can apply the same treatment to any junk cupboard picked up in a market or junk shop.

MATERIALS

wall cabinet
pin hammer
white spirit
steel wool
fine-grade sandpaper
primer
undercoat
eggshell paint
1-inch paint brush
chicken wire from a hardware shop
staple gun or panel pins

HOW TO MAKE

1. Choose a cabinet that has a single central panel in the door. If it is an old cabinet make sure that the door construction is sound. Remove any beading holding the panel in place on the the inside of the door and then carefully knock out the panel by tapping around the edge with a pin hammer. Avoid damaging any beading around the front of the panel by knocking through from the front. If the cabinet has a mirror or window in the door panel, remove the pins holding the glass in place and then very carefully push it out.

2. Prepare all surfaces before painting to ensure they are in the best possible condition. If the cabinet has been waxed, remove the wax coating with white spirit and steel wool, then clean with a rag. Always work in the direction of the grain. If it has been painted before and the paintwork is sound, simply wash it and sand it. If the old paint is chipped or flaking, it is better to strip it off.

3. Apply a coat of primer, then one of undercoat, followed by two coats of eggshell. It is important to sand with fine-grade sandpaper between each coat to give a smooth surface for the next coat.

Remember also to paint all of the inside surfaces, as they will be visible through the chicken wire; painting the shelves a contrasting color, as shown here, is a smart idea.

4. Cut your chicken wire to size using wire cutters. Attach the wire to the reverse side of the cabinet door frame, using a staple gun or panel pins bent over to catch the edges of the wire.

right *Real Forties bathrooms were cold clammy places with peeling linoleum floors and intermittent hot water issued from unpredictable boilers. The sea-green-and-white Long Island bathroom here might be retro in feeling, but is very modern in its comforting supplies of heat and hot water. Simple and functional, it houses a sturdy cast-iron bathtub on ball-and-claw feet, a plain wooden mirrored bath cabinet, and a painted stool for setting down a bathtime drink. Seek out ideas for recreating this relaxed, utilitarian look by rummaging in second-hand stores for big white clinical enamel jugs (the sort that hospitals used for washing babies), old formica or metal-topped tables, metal buckets, and medicine cabinets, or old versions of the wooden bathmat shown below.*

Indispensable for drying big white cotton bath sheets and white rag-rug Portuguese bathmats is my Thirties-style heated chrome towelrod. To finish off my ablutions, I love to wrap up in a soft, white seersucker bathrobe —they're rather expensive, but well worth it for a daily dose of luxury.

Choosing a bathtub is a matter of taste as well as practical consideration. Traditional-style, free-standing cast-iron bathtubs with ball-and-claw feet are deep and look good, but they need sturdy floors to support their weight, the considerable weight of a tubful of water, plus the weight of the bather. In contrast, modern acrylic baths are light, warm to the touch, and come in lots of shapes.

above *Luxurious yet eminently achievable bathroom ideas include a glass candelabra for bathing by candlelight, and a comfortable chair with soft toweling seating. Practical bathroom storage ideas include woven cane laundry baskets and junk objects like old metal school shoe lockers, or tin boxes used to house soaps, lotions, and other paraphernalia.*

Drawstring Bag

A basic bag can be made out of tough cotton and used to store everything from sewing materials to towels. The pattern shown here can be adapted to make roomy laundry bags or sized down to make a trio of practical storage bags for the bathroom. If you want to be really organized you can label utility calico storage bags with indelible fabric pens.

MATERIALS

37 x 45-inch piece heavy cotton

tape measure

pins

scissors

needle

thread

safety pins

sewing machine

HOW TO MAKE

1. For the bag, cut out one piece of fabric measuring 37 × 17 inches. Fold the fabric in half along the length, with right sides together. Pin, baste, and machine stitch one of the long sides for 14 inches, using a seam allowance of ½ inch. Leave a ¾-inch gap and then continue sewing to the end of the seam.

If you want to make a double tie, repeat this process on the second long side. For a single tie only, machine a continuous line of stitching up the other long side. Press the seams open.

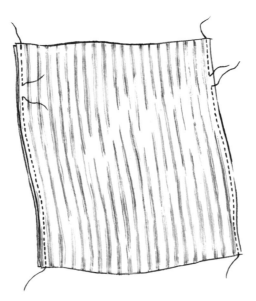

2. To make the casement that will contain the ties, fold over the top raw edge ½-inch all around and press the fold in place. Then fold over a further 2 inches evenly all around, lining up the side seams. Press and pin in position.

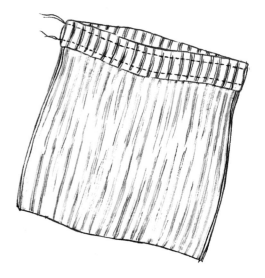

Machine stitch around the hem line, then make a second row of stitching ¾-inch from the folded edge. Turn the bag right side out and press.

3. To make the ties, cut two strips of fabric 1½ x 44 inches. Turn under ¼ inch on all four raw edges on each strip. Fold the strips in half lengthwise and, with wrong sides facing, pin, baste, and machine stitch close to the edge along the open ends and the side.

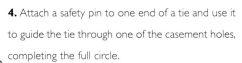

4. Attach a safety pin to one end of a tie and use it to guide the tie through one of the casement holes, completing the full circle.

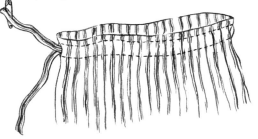

Repeat for the second tie, starting and finishing at the opposite hole. Remove the safety pins, knot the ties, and pull the ends to draw.

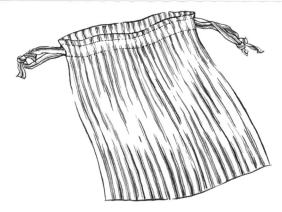

far right *Get the look and create your own Georgian-inspired bathroom with matte eggshell paint, an old-fashioned bathtub on a raised platform, and big weathered brass faucets. Hide elements of contemporary life behind plain paneled closets. Seal wooden floors in matte varnish or use thick cotton bathmats to soak up water from dripping bodies.*

Enameled steel baths are strong and hardwearing (and for this reason favored by hotels and hospitals), but, like modern acrylic baths, they need the support of a frame. For stylish details, either box the bathtub with plain white tiles, or make a border of tongue-and-groove wood panels, which can be painted or waxed for protection.

Bathroom textures and surfaces need to be hardwearing and easy to maintain. Cleaning the bathroom

this page *Old ceramic jugs, weathered wooden shelves with cut-out patterns, cheap painted peg rails, and seashell prints are key elements for a traditional feel.*

right *Daily ablutions are an uplifting experience in this bright and cheery sea-green-and-blue theme. Solid functional fittings that were happily left intact for the owner included a splendid old ceramic sink on a stand with classic faucets, and visible fittings.*

The average bathroom store has a pretty paltry selection of faucets in unremarkable shapes that can be costly. Here are some new ideas:
above *A single stainless-steel spout with an artfully concealed faucet mechanism.*
above right *Brass taps from a builder's yard.*
right *Chunky Victorian pillar faucets found in a salvage yard.*

becomes less work if you wipe bathtubs, washbasins, and showers daily with soapy water while they are still warm, then rinse and dry them; this helps prevent a build-up of dirt. Try not to use abrasive cleaners, which can cause damage to many surfaces and glazes; choose softer sponges or cloths instead.

Ceramic sinks, lavatories, toilets, and shower stalls are widely available and offer a good value. Ceramic tiles for floors and walls provide a good splashproof environment. Well-sealed wooden floors are acceptable, as are terra cotta or linoleum floors, provided they are properly laid to stop water from seeping underneath and causing damage.

this page *Introduce color to bathrooms with bright towels and robes in marine blue and lime green, or deep-blue glass bottles for lotions.*

far right *Swimming pool-inspired tiny blue mosaic tiles are an inventive idea for a walk-in shower space. Equally resourceful are basic stainless-steel kitchen mixer faucets reinvented as a shower spout.*

Avoid carpet—sooner or later it will get wet and will rapidly become moldy and smelly.

When planning a shower, check that you have enough water pressure to produce a powerful downpour. You might need a pump that boosts the flow. Showers can be simple affairs—from a hand set mounted on the bathtub faucet with a protective screen or curtain, to a state-of-the-art walk-in room with a shower that delivers a deluge of water.

There are numerous ways of storing bathroom equipment. Built-in cabinets are useful and should, if possible, be big enough for keeping towels and other bathlinens on hand. Boxes and baskets are good for storing dirty linen, spare towels, toilet brushes, sponges, and other cleaning supplies. Versatile pegs in wood or metal are ideal for hanging make-up bags.

Outdoor Living

When the temperature rises and the days lengthen, images of summer reappear—like dirt between the toes, warm bare skin, icy drinks, and creased cool linen—and it's time to head outside. Dedicated outdoor lovers will already have grabbed the pleasures of those first few tentative days of spring when it's a revelation to see and feel the sun again after months of dreary winter. They pack picnic baskets and blankets and take the first excursion of the season. Given a sunny day and appropriate clothing, I will pack a thermos of hot soup and smoked salmon and cream-cheese bagels and head off with my family to an empty stretch of south coast beach for a picnic.

Then, once summer is well established, there is that feeling that it will go on forever and everyone becomes complacent and irritated with the heat, humidity, and mosquitoes. But when the days are long and the evenings balmy, what a luxury it is to eat breakfast, lunch, and supper *al fresco*. Invigorating as well as relaxing, the event can be as simple as drinking coffee at a sidewalk café—something blissful for city dwellers—or a weekend picnic in the park with the best cheese, bread, and wine that you can afford.

Eating outside is one of life's sensual pleasures. Whatever the scenario, from a windswept beach beneath racing clouds to a warm, flower-scented night, the taste and texture of food seems enchanced when eaten out in the elements. The British, for instance, have always been fond of picnics, packing thermoses, blankets, raincoats, and quantities of ham sandwiches to face unpredictable weather with determination. In complete contrast, Spaniards give in to fiercely hot summer afternoons and laze around shady tables idling over *jamón*, bread, wine, and steaming *paellas* cooked on camping stoves.

The passion for eating *al fresco* has grown with me into adult life. Childhood picnics are remembered for their delicious informality, where for once adults did not bother with knives and forks or insist on elbows being off the table, or even mind if you sprawled out, sandwich in hand. Inspired by books such as Elizabeth David's *Summer Cooking*, my picnics might include French bread soaked with olive oil and garlic, and stuffed with goat's cheese and anchovies. Everything is stored in a plain, but eminently practical ice chest, together with drinks of beer, bubbly wine, or crisp dry Manzanilla sherry.

At home, my tiny backyard becomes an extra room in summer. There is not much sun, but climbing roses and clematis manage to thrive, and flowerpots filled with herbs add color, texture, and culinary detail. As soon as the temperature allows, we set up green metal folding chairs around a big wooden table. I spread the table with white or blue-and-white checked cloths together with jars of roses, nasturtiums, or Queen Anne's lace. In the evening, candles set in flowerpots provide a wonderful glow and do not blow out with every gust of wind.

left *Keep cool with a shady awning made from sheets of cane spread over a simple iron framework. Other ideas for retreating out of the sun include panels of canvas stretched hammock-style across a small courtyard or between trees. For a more permanent arrangement that can be stored over the winter months, invest in a big canvas umbrella. I've seen good ones in basic green-and-white stripes, designed for use on the beach but equally at home in the backyard or country.*

above *The only rule for food served outside is that is should be delicious and easy to eat.*

Restoring Junk Furniture

table

chairs

sandpaper

wire wool

white spirit

hardboard

primer

undercoat

eggshell paint

1-inch paint brush

cotton roller-towel

cotton tape

Just about any old junk furniture can be given a facelift with a coat of paint and some simple covers. I found two wooden chairs and a very battered card table at a local street market and spruced them up with brilliant white eggshell paint.

INSTRUCTIONS

1. Prepare the table and chair surfaces for painting by sanding them with fine abrasive paper. If they have been waxed, clean with white spirit and wire wool, then clean with a rag, always working in the direction of the grain. If they have been painted before yet are in good condition, just wash them down, dry, and sand. If the old paint is flaking or chipped, it is best to strip it off.

2. The card table was bought with a felt top and so I replaced it with a piece of hardboard cut to size and pinned to the frame.

3. Apply primer, then undercoat, followed by two coats of eggshell paint. To ensure a smooth surface for the next coat of paint, finely sand furniture piece after each coat dries.

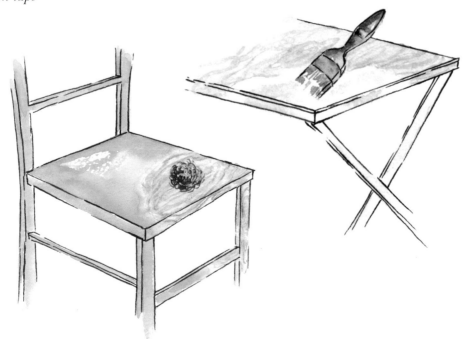

4. For quick and easy chair covers, I used lengths of cotton roller towel. Which comes in finished narrow widths. The material is designed for commercial use and will withstand lots of wear and frequent washing. Measure your lengths so that the cover hangs 6 inches below the seat at the back and front. Fray each of the short cut edges to 1 inch and sew 4 lengths of tape, each 6-inches long, to the roller towel at the points where the seat meets the back. Drape the roller towel over the chair and tie the tapes at the back to secure the cover in place .

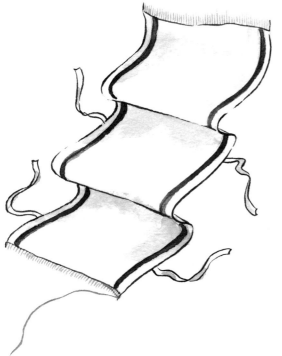

left *Durable, portable, and attractive outdoor ideas: folding wooden tables and chairs (these were borrowed from the local village bar in Spain, but similar ones can be found in secondhand furniture stores); lengths of cotton for tablecloths, pillows for comfort; bright yellow plastic tumblers; woven olive baskets; and jars packed with freshly picked herbs for decoration.*

Sometimes we eat fresh barbecued salmon steaks, sardines, or mackerel stuffed with parsley, lemon, and garlic. For dessert I make strawberry or raspberry ice cream with the help of a small electric ice cream machine and serve it with summer berries and shortcake.

Equipment for eating out in the open has never been so varied. Camping goods outlets are good sources for coolers, stoves, and traditional enamel tin plates and mugs. Sleek, streamlined, shatterproof vacuum flasks are useful for keeping fluids as hot or as cold as you want. Outdoor furniture ideas include fold-up slatted chairs that can be stored away easily in winter. If your budget does not run to an expensive patio table, then cheat with an old door laid across trestles, covered with a cloth in a favorite fabric.

Suppliers

Home

Chambers
P.O. Box 7841,
San Francisco, CA 94120
(mail order)
Everything for the bedroom
and bathrooom.

Crate & Barrel
650 Madison Avenue, New
York, NY 10022
P.O. Box 9059, Wheeling,
Illinois 60090-9059
(mail order)
A wonderful source of good
value furniture and accessories, from simple white
china and glass, to chairs
and beds.

Fish Eddy's
889 Broadway,
New York, NY 10011
Overstock supplies of great
Fifties-style china mugs,
plates, bowls, and so on.

Garnet Hill
P.O. Box 262, Main Street,
Franconia, NH 03580
Bedlinen in natural fibers,
plus wonderful down duvets
and pillows.

Hold Everything
P.O. Box 7807,
San Francisco, CA 94120
Everything for storage from
baskets to shoe holders.

Ikea Long Island
1100 Broadway Mall,
Hicksville, NY 18014
Home basics at great prices,
including assembly kit
furniture and stylish inexpensive kitchenware.

Mombasa Net Canopies
2345 Fort Worth Street,
Grand Prairie, Texas 75050
Mosquito nets to create
romantic bedhangings.

Palecek
P.O. Box 225, Station A,
Richmond, CA 94808
Manufacturers of painted
wicker furniture.

Pier Imports
461 Fifth Avenue,
New York, NY 10017
Great home accessories,
outdoor ideas and furniture.

Portico Bed & Bath
139 Spring Street,
New York, NY 10012
Beautiful white linens, plus
towels and throws.

Pottery Barn
2109 Broadway,
New York, NY 10023
P.O. Box 7044,
San Francisco, CA 94120-
7044 (mail order)
Everything from furniture to
decorating details, such as
muslin curtains, china,
pillows, and candlesticks.

Takashimaya
693 Fifth Avenue,
New York, NY 10012
Exquisite bedlinen, soaps,
and lotions.

**Christian Tortu at
Takashimaya**
693 Fifth Avenue,
New York, NY 10012
A heavenly florist, with cut
flowers, topiary trees, and
delicious scented candles.

**Williamsburg
Catalogue** The Colonial
Williamsburg Foundation,
Department 023,
P.O. Box 3532,
Williamsburg, VA 23187
From simple hurricane lamp
shades to checked blankets.

**Wolfman Gold & Good
Co.** 117 Mercer Street,
New York, NY 10012
Lots of stylish home acces-
sories including china, crisp
linen, and silver flatware.

Fabrics

Laura Ashley
714 Madison Avenue, New
York City, NY 10021
Floral, striped, checked, and
solid cottons in a good
range of colors.

Manuel Canovas
136 East 57th Street,
New York, NY 10022

Stylish floral prints and
woven fabrics in a wide
range of good colors (trade
only—contact for your
nearest distributor)

**Jane Churchill Fabrics &
Wallpaper** at Cowtan &
Tout, 979 Third Avenue,
New York City, NY 10022
Floral, striped, and checked
cotton fabrics (trade only—
contact for your nearest
distributor).

Colefax & Fowler
at Cowtan & Tout,
979 Third Avenue,
New York, NY 10022
Floral printed cottons and
designs in stripes and
checks (trade only—
contact for your nearest
distributor).

Designers Guild at
Osborne & Little,
979 Third Avenue,
New York City, NY 10022
Bright contemporary fabrics
and checked bedlinen
(trade only—contact for
your nearest distributor).

Liberty at Ram, Son, &
Crocker Customer Services
tel 1800-756-7266 (trade
only—contact for your
nearest distributor)
Famous Liberty printed
fabrics, including pretty
floral printed dress lawn.

Marvic Textiles

979 Third Avenue,
New York, NY 10022
A good range of upholstery
textures in smart colorings
(trade only—contact for
your nearest distributor)

Ralph Lauren Home
Collection

980 Madison Avenue,
New York NY 10021
Stylish home accessories,
including smart cotton
fabrics and bedlinen in blue
and white.

Calvin Klein Home

654 Madison Avenue,
New York, NY 10022
Bedlinens and a collection
of plain white china.

Osborne & Little

979 Third Avenue,
New York 10022 (trade
only—contact for your
nearest distributor)
Wide selection of curtain
and upholstery fabrics

Ian Mankin

at Agnes Bourne,
2 Henry Adams Street,
Showroom 220,
San Francisco, CA
9410310022
at Coconut Company,
129-31 Greene Street,
SoHo, New York City,
NY 10012-8080
Great value cottons.

Rosebrand Textiles

517 West 35th Street,
New York, NY
Great value muslin, canvas,
scrim, and ticking.

Sanderson

979 Third Avenue,
New York City, NY 10022
Furnishing fabrics (trade
only—contact for your
nearest distributor)

Food

Dean & Deluca

560 Broadway,
New York NY 10012
A foodhall of epic proportions with everything from
wild mushrooms to coffee.

City Bakery

22 East 17th Street,
New York, NY 10003
Imaginative and delicious
take-out food.

Balducci's

424 6th Avenue,
New York, NY 10012
A wonderful greengrocer,
popular with food stylists.

Modern Furniture

Aero 32 Spring Street,
New York, NY 10012

Wyeth
151 Franklin Street,
New York, NY 10013

Paints

Janovic

30-35 Thompspn Avenue,
Long Island City, NY 11101
Good color range.

Ralph Lauren Paint

980 Madison Avenue,
New York, NY 10021
Vast collection of wonderful
colors, divided into typically
romantic themes, such as
River Rock, and Desert
Hollywood Collection.

Benjamin Moore Paints

Montvale, New Jersey,
New York, NY
Good period-style colors in
muted shades.

Pittsburgh Paints

PPG Industries, Inc.,
1 PPG Place,
Pittsburgh, PA 15272
Good color range.

Pratt & Lambert

75 Townawanda Street,
Buffalo,
New York, NY 142007
Lots of colors, plus good
selection of off-whites.

Secondhand and
Antiques

Ruby Beets Antiques

Poxybogue Road,
Bridgehampton,
New York, NY 11932

Painted furnture, old white
china, and kitchenware.

English Country
Antiques

Snake Hollow Road,
Bridgehampton,
New York, NY 11932
Period country furniture in
pine plus decorative blue-
and-white china.

Hope & Wilder

454 Broome Street,
New York, NY 10013
Decorative old furniture
and accessories.

Sage Street Antiques

Sage Street Harbor,
Long Island, NY
Decorative period furniture
and tableware.

Sammy's

484 Broome Street,
New York, NY
Wide range of junk tables,
chairs, and closets.

Markets

Brimfield Market

Massachusetts
Held the first week of May,
July, and September; great
antique buys, including
china, fabrics, and decorative furniture.

FarmingRon Connecticut

Held in June; great buys.

Credits

Page 1
Checked cotton: Ikea. Jug: Heal's. Tea towels: Crate & Barrel.

Page 2
Walls painted in Benjamin Moore (Nantucket).

Page 6
Plastic bowl: Heal's.

Page 7
Interior design: Susie Manby.

Page 14
Paint swatches from top: Pratt & Lambert, Pearl Lights Designer (White); Pittsburgh, Soft Whites (2510 Milky White); Pittsburgh, Soft Whites (2549 Off White); Pittsburgh, Soft Whites (2523 Golden White); Benjamin Moore, Regal Wall Satin (71 Spanish White); Benjamin Moore, Regal Wall Satin (73 Navajo white). Chair cover fabric: Laura Ashley. Plastic lunch box: Muji. White plates and jugs: Pottery Barn.

Page 15
Ribbed glass: The Conran Shop. Enamel jugs Ruby Beets Antiques. Tea towels: Wolfman Gold & Good Co. Candles: Price's Candles. White bowl: Habitat.

Page 16
Plastic beaker Heal's. Striped table mat: Crate & Barrel.

Page 17
Paint swatches from top: Janovic (2243P Silver Skates); Janovic (2191P Blue Night); Janovic (7235P Blue Lullaby); Janovic (7221P Corner Cupboard);

Janovic (7214T Blue Epic). Plate: Anta. Checked tray: John Lewis.

Page 18
Paint swatches from top: Sanderson Spectrum (41-03 Springtime); Sanderson Spectrum (40-04 Sunny Green); Benjamin Moore Regal Wall Satin (561 Pistachio); Ralph Lauren, Santa Fe Collection (HC-143 Hystorica); Benjamin Moore, Regal Wall Satin (501 Mesquite). Paper napkins: Ikea.

Page 19
Cup and saucer and checked cushion cover: Designers Guild.

Page 20
Lavender paper and folder: Paperchase. Plastic brush: Designers Guild.

Page 21
Paint swatches from top: Benjamin Moore, Regal Wall Satin (1402 Frosted Plum); Ralph Lauren, Santa Fe Collection (SF07C Fresco); Ralph Lauren, Country Collection (C008C Clover Patch); Ralph Lauren, Country Collection (C002B Columbine); Janovic (7194T Lady Di). Bunny chair: Designers Guild. Cushion cover cotton: Manuel Canovas.

Page 22
Paint swatches from top: Pittsburgh, Interiors (3250 Coral Tan); Benjamin Moore, Historic Color Collection (HC-52 Ansonia Peach); Pratt & Lambert (2082 Baccaneet); Dulux (3050-Y50R Free Range); Ralph Lauren, Safari Collection (SA15A Maasai Brick). Terra-cotta pots: Clifton Nurseries.

Page 23–24
Napkins: Habitat. Checked throw: Colefax & Fowler.

Page 25
Paint swatches from top: Pratt & Lambert (1753 Beeswax); Janovic (3042T Dry Bamboo); Benjamin Moore, Historic Color Collection (HC-35 Powell Bluff). Benjamin Moore, Historic Color Collection (HC-9 Chestertown Buff); Pratt & Lambert (2081 Ginger Whip). Chair cover fabric: Habitat. Wall painted in Dulux (Country Cream).

Pages 26–27
Plate: Ruby Beets Antiques.

Page 28
Galvanized metal storage box: Ikea. Wooden and metal flat-ware: Wolfman Gold & Good Co. Pendant light: After Noah.

Page 30
Sisal mat: John Lewis.

Page 34
Plastic yellow bowl: Heal's.

Pages 36–37
From top: First four cotton pieces: Designers Guild; solid green cotton: The Conran Shop; cotton roller towel: Universal Towel Company; cotton: The Conran Shop; cotton mix stripe: John Lewis; cotton ticking: Russell & Chapple; cotton check: Ikea; cotton ticking: Ian Mankin; printed cotton stripe: Laura Ashley.

Pages 38–39
1. Cotton sheeting: John Lewis. 2. Cotton voile: Wolfin Textiles. 3. Cotton: Muriel Short. 4. Polyester/cotton voile: Laura

Ashley. 5. Cotton voile: Wolfin Textiles. 6. Cotton stripe: The Conran Shop. 7. Cotton check: The Conran Shop. 8. Cotton check: The Conran Shop. 9. Cotton gauze: Habitat. 10. Silk: Pongees. 11. Cotton voile check: Habitat. 12. Cotton voile: Laura Ashley. 13. Printed cotton tana lawn: Liberty. 14. Cotton chambray: McCulloch & Wallis. 15. Cotton muslin: Wolfin Textiles. 16. Cotton: Wolfin Textiles. 17 Cotton voile: Muriel Short. 18. Cotton stripe: Ian Mankin. 19. Cotton check: Habitat. 20. Cotton: Designers Guild. 21. Polyester/cotton voile: Laura Ashley. 22. Linen: Wolfin Textiles. 23. Natural linen: Wolfin Textiles. 24. & 25. Cotton voile: Muriel Short. 26. Cotton: The Conran Shop. 27. & 28. Cotton voile check: Designers Guild. 29. Cotton striped voile: Habitat.

Pages 40–41
30. Printed cotton floral/check: Cath Kidston. 31. Wool mix felt: J.W. Bollom. 32. Cotton stripe: The Blue Door. 33. Cotton stripe: Pukka Palace. 34. & 35. Cotton check: Colefax & Fowler. 36 Cotton stripe: The Blue Door. 37. Cotton stripe: Habitat. 38. Cotton chambray: R. Halstuk. 39. Linen check: The Blue Door. 40. Cotton ticking: Ian Mankin. 41. Cotton stripe: The Blue Door. 42. Printed floral cotton: Manuel Canovas. 43. Cotton viscose check: Manuel Canovas. 44. Cotton check: The Blue Door. 45. Cotton stripe: The Malabar Cotton Co. 46. Cotton stripe: Habitat. 47. Printed cotton stripe: Laura Ashley. 48. & 49. Linen herringbone: The Blue Door. 50. 51. 52. & 53. Cotton check: Ian Mankin. 54. Printed cotton

floral: Jane Churchill. 55. Linen: The Blue Door. 56. Cotton check: Habitat. 57. Cotton check: Designers Guild. 58. Cotton check: Ikea. 59. Cotton check: Habitat. 60. Cotton check: Ian Mankin. 61. Cotton check: Designers Guild. 62. Cotton check: Ian Mankin. 63. Cotton check: The Malabar Cotton Co. 64. Cotton check: The Malabar Cotton Co. 65. Cotton drill: Wolfin Textiles. 66. Cotton stripe: Habitat. 67: Cotton roller towel: Universal Towel Company.

Pages 42–43
68. Cotton mix stripe: John Lewis. 69. Cotton denim: Z.Butt Textiles. 70. Cotton ticking: Russell & Chapple. 71. & 72. Cotton: Habitat. 73. Cotton stripe: Designers Guild. 74. Linen: Muriel Short. 75. Cotton muslin: Wolfin Textiles. 76. Cotton: Pierre Frey. 77. Cotton check: Ian Mankin. 78. Check: Ian Mankin. 79. Wool tartan: Anta. 80. Wool check: Anta. 81. Cotton: Osborne & Little. 82. Cotton duck: Russell & Chapple. 83. Cotton canvas: Wolfin Textiles. 84. Cotton gingham daisy: Sanderson. 85. Cotton check: Designers Guild. 86. Cotton check: Habitat. 87. Cotton/viscose: Marvic Textiles. 88. Cotton: Osborne & Little. 89. Cotton: Osborne & Little. 90. Cotton: Osborne & Little. 91. Cotton: The Conran Shop. 92. Cotton check: Designers Guild. 93. Cotton gingham daisy: Sanderson. 94. Cotton check: Habitat. 95. Cotton check: Colefax & Fowler. 96. Linen: Wolfin Textiles.

Pages 44–45
Drawer: Ikea. Chairs (left to

right): Painted in Sanderson Spectrum (39-03 Salad Green Eggshell); covered in Manuel Canovas floral cotton print; painted in Sanderson Spectrum (24-04 Swiss Blue Eggshell); painted in Sanderson Spectrum (21-10 Fidelity)

Page 46
Clockwise from top: Folding chair: The Reject Shop; church chair: Castle Gibson; Bunny chair: Designers Guild; junk shop chair fabric: Cath Kidston; pine occasional table: Ikea; Montecarlo chair: The Conran Shop; birchwood-ply trestle table: McCord; peasant beechwood chair: McCord; stool: Habitat.

Page 47
Clockwise from top: pine dining room table: Ikea; white folding chair: Ikea; metal table: The Conran Shop; wooden kitchen table: Decorative Living; factory chair: After Noah; zinc-top table: Cath Kidston; Nicole chair: Habitat; chair cover fabric: Habitat; table: Ikea painted in Color World (E5-16 Bromel Eggshell) J. W. Bollom.

Page 48
Top: Wrought-iron bed: After Noah. *Left:* Douglas Fir bed in Pawson House, London, designed by John Pawson. *Right:* four-poster bed frame Ikea.

Page 49
Clockwise from top: Chesterfield sofa: A Barn Full of Sofas and Chairs; Coward sofa: SCP; Swedish cot sofa: Sasha Waddell; armchair: George Smith.

Page 50
Cardboard storage boxes: Muji.

Metal mesh wardrobe: Action Handling Equipment. Filing cabinet: B.S. Sales. Chest: local antique shop.

Page 51
Kitchen units: Ikea. Cotton accessory bags: Hold Everything. Wardrobe: local junk shop. Dresser: Colette Aboudaram, France.

Page 52–53
Misu glass tumblers: Ikea. Metal mesh basket: Crate & Barrel.

Page 54
Clockwise from top: Wooden pot stands: Divertimenti; wooden chopping board: Woolworths; gingham knife: Designers Guild; wooden spoons: Divertimenti; glass lemon juicer: Woolworths; corkscrew: Divertimenti; scissors: John Lewis; Sabatier stainless steel knife: Divertimenti; espresso maker: McCord; stainless-steel pedal bin: Divertimenti.

Page 55
Clockwise from top: Le Pentole steamer: Divertimenti; Le Creuset cooking pot: Divertimenti; colander: Wool-worths; fish kettle: Gill Wing; garlic crusher, whisk, lobster crackers: Divertimenti; Le Pentole frying pan: Diverti-menti; kettle: Staines Catering; grater: Divertimenti; sieve: Divertimenti; flatware: McCord.

Page 56
Clockwise from top: Chandelier: Robert Davies; storm lamps: Crate & Barrel; night-lights: Ikea; candle holder: Habitat; paper shade, brass candle holder: The Dining Room Shop; lantern: Habitat.

Page 57
Anglepoise lamp: After Noah. Pendant light: After Noah. Flexi lamp: The Conran Shop.

Page 58
Clockwise from top: Vegetable crates painted in Color World (E9-23 Green): J. W. Bollom; laundry basket: Tobias and the Angel; blanket: Melin Tregwynt; blue-and-green cotton fabric: The Conran Shop; storage chest: Ikea; boxes painted in J. W. Bollom (JWB86 Pottery): Habitat; peg rail: Ikea.

Page 59
Clockwise from top: glass storage jars: Divertimenti; pine cupboard painted in blue eggshell: Ikea; butcher's hooks: Divertimenti; buckets: The Conran Shop and various hardware stores; galvanized steel storage boxes: Muji; shoe rack: Ikea; beaker: Muji; clothes-rod: B.S. Sales; shoe boxes covered in Manuel Canovas checked fabric.

Page 60
Picture frames: Ikea.

Page 61
Plates: English Country Antiques. Beechwood picture frames: Habitat. Bowls: Divertimenti. Shadow boxes: Habitat.

Page 62
Clockwise from top: mug Habitat; tartan plate: Anta; white coffee cup and saucer: Habitat; blue-and-white china: Crate & Barrel; dinner plate: Heal's; champagne flute: The Conran Shop; Duralex tumbler: local Spanish super-market; ripple glass: Designers Guild; tumbler: Crate & Barrel; tumbler: Pottery Barn; Misu

tumbler: Ikea; Cornishware plate: Heal's.

Page 63
Clockwise from top: gingham bowl: McCord; jug: Divertimenti; blue-and-white bowl: Habitat; spotty bowl: Designers Guild; cream cup & saucer: Veronique Pichon at Designers Guild; white plate: Wedgwood; Poole pottery jug: Designers Guild.

Pages 66–67
Enamel jug: Ruby Beets Antiques.

Pages 68–69
Saucepans: Brick Lane Market. Tartan plates: Anta. Sink and faucets: Aston Matthews.

Pages 70–71
Swedish stove: Jotul. Interior design: Susie Manby. Trug: Clifton Nurseries.

Pages 72–73
Cans: painted in Farrow & Ball (44 Cream Eggshell). Crates painted in J.W. Bollom Color World (E6-46 Yellow, E9-23 Green, & JWB86 Blue). Flowerpots painted in J.W. Bollum (White matte emulsion) and Sanderson Spectrum (Lavender Lave 21-17 Vinyl matte emulsion).

Pages 74–75
Mason jars: After Noah. Cake tins: Brick Lane Market. White metal chair: Brimfield Market.

Pages 76–77
Carrara marble counter, sink and spout, white lacquered mdf cupboards and drawer units in Pawson House, London: all designed by John Pawson. Pasta pan: Divertimenti.

Pages 78–79
Cotton chair cover fabric: similar may be found at Universal Towel Company. White bowls: Wolfman Gold & Good Co.

Page 80
Below left: Provençal chairs: Parisian junk shop.

Page 81
Table and dining-room chairs: similar may be found at After Noah. Flowerpots Clifton Nurseries. White china: Gill Wing.

Pages 82–83
Calico chair cover fabric: Russell & Chapple. Metal table: The Conran Shop. Curtain fabric: Designers Guild. White plates: Wedgwood. Walls painted in Sanderson Spectrum (Fascination 2309M).

Pages 86–87
Left: Wicker parlor chairs: Palecek. Myrtle topiary: Christian Tortu at Takashimaya. White table: local junk shop. *Right*: Laminated table and Tulip chair: Frank Lord.

Pages 88–89
Left and top right: room and furniture in Pawson House, London, designed by John Pawson. *Below right*: loft dining area by James Lynch.

Pages 90–91
Shades in cotton check: Colefax & Fowler. Checked plastic table-cloth: John Lewis. Wool throw: Anta. Chandelier: Robert Davies. Walls painted in Dulux (Country Cream Eggshell).

Pages 92–93
Sofa fabric: Sanderson. Green

cotton check pillow: Laura Ashley. Pillow in blue cotton: The Conran Shop. Pillows in blue check: JAB. Wool throw: Anta.

Pages 94–95
Fabric swatches on left: Narrow and wide cotton stripes: Habitat; Cotton check: The Conran Shop. *Center*: Floral cotton covers, striped cotton drapes, linen and cotton rug: Ralph Lauren; ticking cushion fabric: Ralph Lauren and antique samples. *Right*: metal daybed: Colette Aboudaram, France; antique ticking fabric on pillows: Bryony Thomasson.

Page 96
Chair and sofa cover, cotton rug, and paint: Ralph Lauren. Pillowcover fabric: Designers Guild.

Page 97
Left: Paint: Farrow & Ball (Mix of Olive and Calke Green matte emulsions); candle holder and side cupboard: After Noah; *Right*: Blue cotton sofa fabric: The Conran Shop, Paris; terra-cotta cotton armchair fabric: Ian Mankin; interior design: Susie Manby.

Pages 98–99
Butler's tray table painted in Sanderson Spectrum (50-23 Satinwood): Crate & Barrel. *Center*: Drapes in checked cotton: Designers Guild; wing chair covered in Tulipan: Marvic Textiles; cream paint: Dulux (Buttermilk); white table: Brick Lane market. *Right*: Checked terra-cotta fabric on sofa: Manuel Canovas; wooden chest and metal planter: Tobias and The Angel.

Pages 100–101
Cotton muslin: Wolfin Textiles.

Page 102
Top: Sofa: Nick Plant. *Left*: light: Lieux, Paris. wool appliqué cover: Siécle, Paris. *Right*: basket chair: Alfies Antique Market; mirror: Cligoncourt Market, Paris.

Page 103
Wall painted in Benjamin Moore (Nantucket).

Pages 104–105
Main picture: Wool blankets: Anta; cotton rugs: Habitat; cupboard: Ikea; checked cotton chair covers: Ian Mankin; chairs: A Barn Full of Sofas and Chairs; chandelier: Wilchester Counyt; pleated shades: The Dining Room Shop.

Pages 106–109
Cotton drill: Z. Butt Textiles.

Pages 110–111
Left: Chair in antique ticking: Bryony Thomasson; interior design: Susie Manby. *Centre*: sofa: Ikea. *Right*: filing cabinet: B.S.Sales; trestle table: McCord; filing boxes and frames: Ikea;. metal chair and cover in cotton check: Habitat; Bunny chair: Designers Guild; wastebasket: The Conran Shop.

Page 112
Left: Curtain fabric: The Conran Shop.

Page 113
Linen curtain fabric: Rosebrand Textiles. Myrtle tree: Christian Tortu at Takashimaya. Sofa: local barn sale. Walls painted in Benjamin Moore (Nantucket).

Page 118
Bed: Portobello Road Market. Chair: Alfies Antique Market. White paint: John Oliver.

Page 119
Old linen: Judy Greenwood.

Pages 120–21
Cotton stripe: Laura Ashley.

Page 122
Table: Colette Aboudaram, France.

Page 123
Striped cotton pillowcase: Ralph Lauren. Quilt bedspread: Ruby Beets Antiques. Hanging quilt: Brimfield Market.

Page 124
Mosquito net: Mombasa Net Canopies.

Page 125
Tom Dixon light: Gladys Mougin, Paris. Indian cotton bedspread: Living Tradition, Paris.

Page 126
Bolster pad: John Lewis. Cotton striped fabric: Laura Ashley. Wooden box: Tobias and The Angel.

Page 127
Bed: Jim Howitt. Antique quilt: Judy Greenwood. Pillowcases in cotton lawn: Liberty. Linen fabric on seat cushions: Laura Ashley. White bedlinen: John Lewis. Paint: Dulux (Sandstone Eggshell).

Page 128
Muslin curtains: Pottery Barn. Bedlinen: Designers Guild. Wool blanket: Melin Tregwynt.

Page 129
Bunkbeds: Habitat, Paris.

Page 132
Left: shower curtain: Similar found at Crate & Barrel. *Below right*: Drawstring bag fabric: Russell & Chapple. Starfish: Eaton Shell Shop.

Page 133
Antique cupboard: Colette Aboudaram, France. Interior design: Susie Manby.

Pages 134–35
Bathroom cupoard, painted in Sanderson Spectrum (Beryl Green 35-16): Ikea.

Page 136
Wooden duckboard: Habitat.

Page 137
Left: Peg rail: Robert Davies. Chair: Alfies Antique Market. *Top right*: Shoe rack, pine mirror, butcher's hooks: After Noah; Brushes, soaps: The Conran Shop; towels: Muji; galvanized bucket: The Conran Shop; medicine bottles: local junk shop. *Bottom right*: linen basket: Habitat.

Pages 138–39
Cotton ticking: Russell & Chapple. Tea towels: Divertimenti.

Page 140
Jug: Sage Street Antiques. Peg rail: Ikea.

Page 141
Faucets and bath: Lassco. Wooden bath rack: Habitat. Cotton towels: John Lewis.

Page 141–43
Nail brush: John Lewis. *Top left*: Faucet and stone basin in

Pawson House, London: designed by John Pawson. *Top right*: Outdoor brass faucets from builders' merchants. *Bottom*: faucets and bath: Lassco; bath rack: Habitat.

Page 144
Left: towels, flannels, and robe: Designers Guild. *Right*: towels: John Lewis.

Page 145
Bathroom: James Lynch. Bath: Lassco. Shower faucets: Nicholls and Clarke. Cans: Alfies Antique Market.

Pages 146–47
Flatware: Designers Guild. Beaker: Heal's. Blanket: Anta. Table: Brick Lane Market.

Page 149
Tablecloth fabric: Designers Guild. Chair and table: Clifton Nurseries.

Pages 150–51
Cotton roller towel: Universal Towel Company

Page 153
Beakers: Heal's. Tablecloth fabric and pillows: Designers Guild.

Acknowledgments

I want to say a huge thank you to **Jacqui Small, Anne Ryland, David Peters, Sian Parkhouse, Sophie Pearse, Penny Stock, Janet Cato** and everyone at **RPS**, who have worked like Trojans to produce *Pure Style*.

I am indebted to **Henry Bourne**, whose stunning photographs have captured the spirit of the book so perfectly.

I would also like to thank **Nick Pope** for the excellent cut-out photography.

Many, many thanks to my assistant **Fiona Craig-McFeely**, who has been an invaluable source of efficiency and support.

Thanks to **Tessa Brown** for making up the soft furnishing projects, and to **Jacqueline Pestell** for illustrating them.

I would like to thank the following people for allowing us to photograph their homes for inclusion in *Pure Style* : **Shiraz Maneksha; Ilse Crawford; James Lynch** and **Sian Tucker; John** and **Catherine Pawson, The Pawson House, London; Marie Kalt; John** and **Claudia Brown; Peri Wolfman** and **Charles Gold, Wolfman Gold & Good Co.; Tricia Foley; Ellen O'Neill; Mary Emmerling; Gary Wright** and **Sheila Teague**.

My family have been unfailingly supportive, and have put up with many months of upheaval. Big hugs for my husband **Alastair**, my children **Tom, Georgia** and **Grace**, and my mother and father.

Index